DRONES:
THEIR MANY CIVILIAN USES AND THE U.S. LAWS SURROUNDING THEM

D1469151

Jonathan B. Rupprecht, Esq.

DRONES:
THEIR MANY CIVILIAN USES
AND
THE U.S. LAWS SURROUNDING
THEM

Warnings and Legal Disclaimer:

"This publication is designed to provide accurate and authoritative information in regard to the subject matter covered. It is provided with the understanding that the publisher is not engaged in rendering legal, accounting, or other professional services. If legal advice or other professional assistance is required, the services of a competent professional person should be sought."-*From a Declaration of Principles jointly adopted by a committee of the American Bar Association and a committee of Publishers and Associations.*

Sources

Because the internet is constantly changing, any web address in this book might have changed since it was written.

Many thanks to Brent Dillon for the picture on the front cover.

Reviews

"This book is an interesting read and worth the investment."

-**Patrick Egan**, Host and Executive Producer of the sUAS News Podcast Series and Drone TV at sUAS News, worked on the first FAA Aviation Rules Committee on UAS.
www.suasnews.com

"Great overview of the FAA regulations, or lack thereof, pertaining to unmanned aerial systems. A must-read for anyone contemplating entering this arena,"

-**Gus Calderon**, Founder of Airspace Consulting and commercial pilot.
www.airspaceconsulting.com

"It's not all about Amazon deliveries! The author reviews the different applications for unmanned aerial systems as well as the legal challenges that have handicapped the industry for so many years. Excellent reference material,"

-**Maha Calderon**, Certified Flight Instructor, Director of Civilian Drones: Search and Rescue.
www.civiliandronesmovie.com

"A comprehensive field guide to hunting UAV law in the wild west of unmanned systems."

-**Timothy Takahashi**, J.D./Ph.D, Professor of Practice - Aerospace Engineering, School for Engineering of Matter, Transport and Energy, Arizona State University

"In the current state of UAS policy, operators have confusing and sometimes conflicting information. In this book, Jonathan provides clear guidance for the safe and legal operation of UAS in the current state of affairs. The FAA process is demystified. As the CEO of a UAS integration company, I recommend this book to clients, colleagues, and anyone interested in operating UAS in a safe and legal manner."

    -Brock Christoval, CEO & Founder of Flyspan Systems, Inc.www.flyspansystems.com, @Flyspan

"Great book with tons of sources! I will definitely use this book as a resource of sources for building and managing training and operational programs in the future. It is extremely helpful to have good resources when creating programs of instruction, technical manuals, and other relevant documentation for UAS programs I am managing."

    -Nicholas Damron, U.S. Army UAS Instructor (8 years of flight training and operational experience). www.linkedin.com/in/theunmannedadvocate @Unmanned_Adv

CONTENTS

About the Author

Jonathan B. Rupprecht is a lawyer and a commercial pilot with single-engine, multi-engine, and instrument ratings. He is also an airplane flight instructor and instrument flight instructor. Jonathan obtained a Bachelor of Science in Professional Aeronautics from Embry-Riddle Aeronautical University, Magna Cum Laude, and a Juris Doctor from Florida International University School of Law. He has conducted extensive research on the integration of unmanned aircraft into the Japanese airspace compared to the integration in the United States' airspace. From that research, Jonathan authored this book. He later was an adviser for one of the amicus briefs for the highly publicized *Huerta v. Pirker* case. Jonathan is a co-author on an American Bar Association book called *Unmanned Aircraft in the National Airspace: Critical Issues, Technology, and the Law.* Jonathan wrote on administrative law, the FAA rule making process, the special rule on unmanned aircraft, and a brief history of unmanned aircraft.

Jonathan is currently practicing law at his firm Rupprecht Law, P.A. (www.jrupprechtlaw.com) in South Florida. Jonathan is open to any comments, questions, or suggestions and can be contacted at jon@jrupprechtlaw.com

CHAPTER ONE: WHY YOU SHOULD READ THIS BOOK

The media has been buzzing about Amazon's announcement of their plans to use drones to deliver packages to customers.[1] Soon after Amazon made their announcement, DHL[2] and UPS[3] followed with their own drone delivery announcements. Google has also become interested in drones as evidenced by their purchase of Titan Aerospace.[4] These activities have caused many people to wonder what is going on with integration which is why I wrote this book. This book was written to be a useful resource for hobbyists, lawyers,

---

[1] *See Amazon Prime Air*, http://www.amazon.com/b?node=8037720011 (last visited Jan. 21, 2015).

[2] *See* Gary Mortimer, *DHL drone delivers medicine across the Rhine*, SUAS NEWS (Jan. 9, 2014), http://www.suasnews.com/2014/01/26865/dhl-drone-delivers-medicine-across-the-rhine/.

[3] *See* Joanna Stern, *Like Amazon, UPS Also Considering Using Unmanned Flying Vehicles*, ABC NEWS (Dec. 3, 2013), http://abcnews.go.com/Technology/amazon-ups-drone-delivery-options/story?id=21086160.

[4] *See* Hayley Tsukayama, *Google buys drone maker Titan Aerospace*, WASHINGTON POST (April 15, 2014), http://www.washingtonpost.com/blogs/the-switch/wp/2014/04/14/google-buys-drone-maker-titan-aerospace-2/

businessmen, or anyone wanting to know what is going on legally to integrate what are called unmanned aircraft, "drones," or remotely piloted aircraft into the United States' airspace. While many individuals have been talking about the Fourth Amendment concerns with unmanned government aircraft (public unmanned aircraft),[5] this book does not focus on those privacy concerns. This book will give an overview about unmanned aircraft and then explore their uses. Finally, this book will dive into the statutes, regulations, and policy statements surrounding unmanned aircraft.

---

[5] *See* John Villasenor, *Observations from Above: Unmanned Aircraft Systems and Privacy*, 36 HARV. J.L. & PUB. POL'Y 457 (2013).

CHAPTER TWO: BRIEF OVERVIEW OF UNMANNED AIRCRAFT

B ecause many countries are using different terms, there needs to be a common understanding of what these drone aircraft are called and how they will be referred to in this book.

A. DEFINITIONS

There are many abbreviations in this industry, more than a can of alphabet soup. Unmanned aircraft ("UA") are flying machines without any pilot on board.[6] UA, Unmanned Aerial Vehicles ("UAV's"), "drones," Remotely Piloted Aircraft ("RPA"), Remotely Piloted Vehicles ("RPV"), and Remotely Piloted Air System are all used

---

[6] *See* Bart Elias, CONG. RESEARCH SERV., R42718, PILOTLESS DRONES: BACKGROUND AND CONSIDERATIONS FOR CONGRESS REGARDING UNMANNED AIRCRAFT OPERATIONS IN THE NATIONAL AIRSPACE SYSTEM 1 n. 1 (2012), *available at* http://www.fas.org/sgp/crs/natsec/R42718.pdf ("Unmanned aerial vehicles (UAVs) refer to the unmanned aircraft in these systems, which are often referred to as drones in the media. The terms UAVs, unmanned aircraft, and drones are used interchangeably throughout this report.").

somewhat synonymously in the media, public, and in the government around the world. Some people also use the term UAV's to describe UA but this term should not be used in the United States because it is a legally incorrect term. Generally, the term "vehicle" describes a conveyance that provides transportation on the ground while the term "aircraft" describes a conveyance providing transportation in the air.[7] Because many nations and organizations are all using a variety of different names to describe the same things, there is not one specific, correct term used for this type of aircraft.

One argument for the use of the term RPA is that the term UA is an umbrella term for *any* unmanned aircraft and that one of the subcategories of UA is called remotely *piloted* aircraft.[8] According to that argument, the RPA designation means that there is a pilot outside

---

[7] *See United States v. Reid*, 206 F. Supp. 2d 132, 138-42 (D. Mass. 2002)(concluding why the term "vehicle" does not encompass aircraft based in part upon many sections in the United States Code using the terms "vehicle" and "aircraft" distinctly from one another.); 1 U.S.C. § 4("The word "vehicle" includes every description of carriage or other artificial contrivance used, or capable of being used, as a means of transportation on land."); 49 U.S.C. § 40102(a)(6)("'[A]ircraft' means any contrivance invented, used, or designed to navigate, or fly in, the air.").

[8] *See* Int'l Civil Aviation Org. [ICAO], *Unmanned Aircraft Systems (UAS)*, at x, Cir. 328-AN/190 (1st ed. 2011), *available at* http://www.icao.int/Meetings/UAS/Documents/Circular%20328_en.pdf ("Remotely-piloted aircraft. An aircraft where the flying pilot is not on board the aircraft. Note.— This is a subcategory of unmanned aircraft.").

the aircraft actively controlling the RPA as opposed to a pilot pre-programming a UA to run a mission before it takes off.

When you take a UA and combine it with ground communications equipment, some radio frequencies (data link), and a pilot, you have a complete operating package called an unmanned aerial system ("UAS") [9] or what the International Civil Aviation Organization ("ICAO") calls a Remotely Piloted Aircraft System ("RPAS"). [10] Remember RPA and RPAS are just like UA and UAS. The Federal Aviation Administration ("FAA"), the U.S. Department of Defense ("DOD"), and the European Aviation Safety Agency ("EASA") are using the term UAS. [11] Time will tell what the correct terms are globally but in this book the term UA and UAS will be used instead of RPA or RPAS.

---

[9] *See* Elias, *supra* note 6, 1 n1.

[10] *See* ICAO, *Manual on Remotely Piloted Aircraft Systems (RPAS)*, at 2, ICAO Doc. 22 (1st ed. 2012), *available at* http://adsb.tc.faa.gov/ICAO-ASP/ASP12-Montreal-12/IP%20ASP12-12-Draft%20RPAS%20Manual.pdf ("A remotely-piloted aircraft, its associated remote pilot station(s), the required command and control links and any other components as specified in the type design.").

[11] KONSTANTINOS DALAMAGKIDIS ET AL., ON INTEGRATING UNMANNED AIRCRAFT SYSTEMS INTO THE NATIONAL AIRSPACE SYSTEM 2-3 (Tzafestas ed., 2nd ed. 2012).

6

B. UA HAVE MANY USES

UA have a variety of uses and have been put into service for a long

time. Being used as far back as during World War II, the U.S. military

developed a system where a manned bomber plane would remotely

control another unmanned bomber to crash into enemy targets after the

pilot of the unmanned plane had parachuted out. The future U.S.

President John F. Kennedy's older brother died when the aircraft he

was flying blew up before he had a chance to parachute out of the

bomber in route to attack a Nazi super cannon as a UA.[12] There is also

a laundry list of uses of where UA are a cost effective[13] means to

solving problems. In agriculture, they can be used for crop dusting,[14]

---

[12] *See* Anthony Leviero, *Kennedy Jr. Died In Air Explosion*, N.Y. TIMES, Oct. 25th, 1945, *available at* http://select.nytimes.com/gst/abstract.html?res=FB0B11FB3D5E1B7B93C7AB178 BD95F418485F9 (requires subscription or individual payment for article); *see also* Trevor Jermy, *Lt. Joe Kennedy*, NORFOLK AND SUFFOLK AVIATION MUSEUM, http://www.aviationmuseum.net/JoeKennedy.htm

[13] Villasenor, *supra* note 5, at 467 ("Ben Miller, the Unmanned Aircraft Program Manager [at the Sherriff's Office] in Mesa County[, Colorado], puts the per-hour operating cost of Mesa County's UAS at $25 . . . .").

[14] *See Unmanned Drones Used For Spraying To Better Assist Crop Growth*, CBS Sacramento (June 9, 2013 11:05 PM), http://sacramento.cbslocal.com/2013/06/09/unmanned-drones-used-for-spraying-to-better-assist-crop-growth/ ("'Ken Giles, a UC Davis engineer professor' says that 'drones are already being commercially used by about 2,500 operators in Japan.'").

fertilizing crops, and monitoring growth.[15] In firefighting, they can be used to give instant aerial images of what the fire is doing.[16] They can be used to track invasive plants and animals in forest management.[17] Geological surveying, real estate property viewing, emergency communications relief, pipe line monitoring, power line monitoring, and radiation monitoring[18] are many examples of how UA can be used.[19] One school created a list with as many as 300 different mission types.[20]

Civilian Uses

-Survey, Maintenance, and Management- Crop Monitoring, Pesticide or Herbicide Spraying, Real Estate Advertising, Mineral, Fisheries, Wildlife, Weather or Atmosphere, Ice Flow, Aerial

---

[15] *See ING Robotic Aviation Pitches Responder Robotic Aircraft at TFI World Fertilizer Conference*, UAS VISION (Sept. 13, 2013), http://www.uasvision.com/2013/09/24/ing-robotic-aviation-pitches-responder-robotic-aircraft-at-tfi-world-fertilizer-conference/ (last visited Jan. 21, 2015).
[16]*See FAA Cuts the Red Tape to Let UAS Work Yosemite Wildfire*, FED. AVIATION ADMIN. (Sept. 6, 2013), http://www.faa.gov/news/updates/?newsId=73720
[17] *See* Ryan Becker, *Aerial Vegetation Survey*, U.S. DEPT. OF AGRIC., http://www.fs.fed.us/t-d/programs/im/aerial/uav.shtml
[18]*See Radiation Surveillance and Unmanned Aerial Vehicles*, RADIATION AND NUCLEAR SAFETY AUTH. OF FIN., www.stuk.fi/julkaisut_maaraykset/en_GB/stuk-ttl-flyers/_files/88555484220687337/default/Flyer_008_Radiation_surveillance_and_U AVs.pdf
[19] *See Applications*, BARNARDMICROSYSTEMS.COM, http://www.barnardmicrosystems.com/UAV/applications/applications.html
[20] *See Commercial Applications*, UNMANNED VEHICLE UNIVERSITY, http://www.uxvuniversity.com/careers/

Photo, Power or Pipeline, Imagery, Mapping, Pollution, and Oceanography.

-Communications- Media, News, and Advertising.

Government Uses

-Border or Coastal Patrol- Counter Smuggling, Anti-Terrorism, and Port Security.

-Law Enforcement or Emergency Response- Forest Fires, Search & Rescue, SWAT, Fire Rescue, Policing, Surveillance, Traffic, and Missing Persons.

C. UA WILL HAVE A MASSIVE ECONOMIC IMPACT

UA will have an economic impact by creating jobs and revenue, reducing operating costs that farmers already have by providing precision agriculture spraying and data, and providing first responders with lower cost solutions for rescue operations.

1. UA WILL CREATE JOBS AND REVENUE

The economic impacts of UA usage and implementation will be massive. The Association for Unmanned Vehicle Systems

International ("AUVSI") created an economic report[21] declaring that "[t]he economic impact of the integration of [UAV's] into the [US airspace] will total more than $13.6 billion [] in the first three years of integration and will grow sustainably for the foreseeable future, cumulating to more than $82.1 billion between 2015 and 2025 . . . ."[22] The report also stated that UA "will create more than 34,000 manufacturing jobs [] and more than 70,000 new jobs in the first three years" with estimated tax revenue of "$482 million in the first 11 years following integration."[23] The most impacting statement in the report was "[e]very year that integration is delayed, the United States loses more than *$10 billion* in potential economic impact. This translates to a loss of *$27.6 million per day that UAS are not integrated into the NAS*."[24]

The Teal Group also created a world market study for the 2013, and reported that "current worldwide UA expenditures of $5.2 billion

---

[21] Darryl Jenkins et. al., *The Economic Impact Of Unmanned Aircraft Systems Integration In The United States*, ASS'N. FOR UNMANNED VEHICLE SYS. INT'L., 1 (Mar. 2013), *available at* http://higherlogicdownload.s3.amazonaws.com/AUVSI/958c920a-7f9b-4ad2-9807-f9a4e95d1ef1/UploadedImages/New_Economic%20Report%202013%20Full.pdf

[22] *Id.* at 2.

[23] *Id.*

[24] *Id.*

annually to $11.6 billion, totaling just over $89 billion in the next ten years."[25] Not only will jobs and revenue be created from U.S. demand, but also there will be demand from overseas interests.

Precision agriculture will be the largest market for UA sales. The AUVSI report forecasted the 2015 total U.S. economic impact of agricultural spending to be about $2.1 billion[26] and the public sector spending impact of about $89.9 million.[27]

2. UA WILL REDUCE COSTS FOR FARMERS AND PROVIDE SERVICES TO FARMERS

Farmers will stand to gain the first benefits of UA technology, not by increasing production but by decreasing spending on operations.

a. UA Will Provide Valuable Images To Monitor Crops

---

[25] Press Release, Teal Group Corp., Teal Group Predicts Worldwide UAV Market Will Total $89 Billion in Its 2013 UAV Market Profile and Forecast (June 13, 2013), http://tealgroup.com/index.php/about-teal-group-corporation/press-releases/94-2013-uav-press-release

[26] Jenkins, *supra* note 21, at 13.

[27] Jenkins, *supra* note 21, at 20.

Farmers are eager to start using UA to take images of their crops.[28] Farmers can obtain images of their crops by LandSat,[29] private satellites, traditional piloted aircraft, or UA. The major problems are that the private satellites and piloted aircraft are expensive and LandSat and the private satellites do not have good resolution. On top of the bad resolution, if the farmer has clouds over his fields, he will have to wait until the satellite orbits back around to his field to get new images which can take more than two weeks. Once a UA is purchased, fuel or electricity to power the UA and regular maintenance are the only operating costs the farmer would need. The big issues are not in obtaining the images but in interpreting the images so that a farmer knows how to treat the problems with his crops. Data interpretation will be a big need for farmers.

What makes UA better than these other alternatives is that certain sensors can detect signs of crop health that are not readily seen by the naked eye. This reason is why the University of Kansas is working

---

[28] *See Drones Special - Part 1*, AGRICULTURE.COM, http://www.agriculture.com/videos/v/76090696/drones-special-part-1.htm?sssdmh=dm17.675802

[29] *See Landsat Project Description*, U.S. GEOLOGICAL SURVEY, http://landsat.usgs.gov/about_project_descriptions.php (stating "moderate-resolution").

with infrared sensors on UA to detect drought-stressed soybeans. [30] In the near future, a farmer will have the ability to scan his fields with one of these UA, know exactly where the problems are, and have the option to water the plants accordingly. He can also use a UA to spray nutrients or herbicide on the areas detected to help the crop.

In addition to detecting stressed plants, the University of Florida is working on detecting citrus canker, a disease that attacks orange trees, using tractor-based sensors along with a UA that monitors the canopy of the trees from above with sensors. [31] There is also work going on using UA to detect grapevine trunk disease. [32]

b. UA Will Provide More Precise Spraying While Reducing Spraying Costs

Precision watering is important in farm lands in the western regions of the U.S. where water is a precious comodity. Currently,

---

[30] *See* Kevin Price & Deon van der Merwe, *Small Unmanned Aircraft Systems for crop and grassland monitoring*, KANSAS STATE UNIVERSITY EXTENSION AGRONOMY E-UPDATE, 4 (April 5, 2013), http://www.agronomy.k-state.edu/documents/eupdates/eupdate040513.pdf

[31] *See* Reza Ehsani & Sindhuja Sankara, *Sensors and sensing technologies for Disease Detection*, UNIV. OF FLA., 2 (June, 2010), http://www.crec.ifas.ufl.edu/extension/trade_journals/2010/2010%20June%20sensoring%20technology.pdf

[32] *See* Mark Sosnowski, *Final Report To Grape And Wine Research & Development Corporation*, 9 (July 31, 2012), http://www.gwrdc.com.au/wp-content/uploads/2012/09/GWT-1113.pdf

farmers have to use more water than they actually need because (1) they can not detect which areas of their crops are stressed, and (2) the cost of overwatering the fields is cheaper than not watering and losing an entire crop.[33] Knowing where *not* to spray will reduce the overall water usage in farms.

Precision herbicide spraying is just as important as watering. Yamaha has been producing UA helicopters for agriculture spraying purposes since 1991. Steve Markofski, who works for Yamaha here in the U.S. said, "Tractors, traditionally used in Napa vineyards, can spray about two acres an hour, but RMAX can do 12 to 15 acres an hour. And with RMAX . . . there's no soil compaction, no crop damage, the operator is not exposed to chemicals and it is safer, because he doesn't have to drive in challenging terrain, like slippery hills."[34]

---

[33] *See* Gary Mortimer, *Chris Anderson sUAS*, YouTube (Sept. 8, 2013), http://www.youtube.com/watch?v=0Mdr7x6bAQc&list=UUV1eWkyxMj35eEsPKrpz

[34] Rich Tuttle, *Flight Plan for UAVs*, PrecisionAG, http://www.precisionag.com/equipment/flight-plan-for-uavs/

While UA will provide more spraying, they will also reduce unneeded spraying. Chris Anderson of 3D Robotics explains this good point,

> [H]alf of the inputs that we put into agriculture are wasted. We are spraying too much or we are spraying too little. We are spraying the wrong places. We are using too much water. Why are we doing this? Because the cost of using too little is really high. The cost of missing a disease outbreak is the loss of the entire crop so we prophylactically spray ahead of time. We spray fungicide in June because fungal infections happen in July. Do you have a fungal infection? Don't know. If you did have a fungal infection, where is the fungal infection? Don't know. You just spray everywhere to insure this doesn't happen.[35]

3. UA WILL SAVE LIVES

UA are ideal for search and rescue ("SAR") missions. Canada has already been integrating UA. In May 2013, the Royal Mounted Police could not find a man, who was lost after sustaining a head injury from a car crash, using a search and rescue *manned* helicopter but they did find the lost man after using a UA.[36] A documentary called "Civilian

---

[35] *See* Mortimer, *supra* note 33, at 9:29.
[36] *See* John Weidlich, *Aerial drone locates Sask. man injured in rollover crash*, CBC NEWS (May 09, 2013 4:23 PM CT), http://www.cbc.ca/news/canada/saskatchewan/aerial-drone-locates-sask-man-injured-in-rollover-crash-1.1398942

Drones- Search And Rescue"[37] detailed one striking instance in the U.S. when Gene Robinson, who runs a 501(c)(3) organization called RP Search Services [38] was involved in a massive search for a small boy along with the Texas Rangers, the Liberty County Texas Sheriff Department, volunteers, and *manned* helicopters; when everyone was packing up to finally leave and end the search, Gene started searching with his UA and found the boy.[39]

With all of these wonderful applications, many questions are raised. How are UA to be kept from crashing into each other or into manned airplanes? How are airplanes with no pilots on board supposed to see and avoid crashing into other aircraft? Furthermore, these questions are not fanciful. In the last few years, even more questions have been raised based upon the accident records of UA.

---

[37] *See* Gary Mortimer, *Civilian Drones Search and Rescue*, YouTube (Nov 3, 2013), http://www.youtube.com/watch?v=vowfpS--rj0&feature=c4-overview&list=UUV1eWkyxMj35eEsPKrpzJrQ

[38] RP SEARCH SERVICES, http://rpsearchservices.org/ (last visited Jan. 21, 2015).

[39] *See* Mortimer, *supra* note 37, at 10:38; *see also* Gary Mortimer, *UAS operator finds body of missing Texas boy*, SUAS NEWS, http://www.suasnews.com/2012/04/14210/uas-operator-finds-body-of-missing-texas-boy/

What if the UA is going to crash,[40] the engine stops working,[41] the UA has an electrical failure,[42] or the radio controls stop working?[43] How do you prevent a UA pilot from accidentally starting his UA and crashing it into a parked cargo plane,[44] or prevent the UA from having a midair collision with a flying C-130?[45] What about preventing the worst scenario of all, a UA crashing into a passenger jet full of

---

[40] *See* Martin Weil, *Drone crashes into Virginia bull run crowd*, THE WASHINGTON POST, http://articles.washingtonpost.com/2013-08-26/local/41446472_1_drone-tomato-fight-public-event, (UA crashes into a crowd during an event).

[41] *See Executive Summary Aircraft Accident Investigation*, U.S. AIR FORCE, http://usaf.aib.law.af.mil/ExecSum2012/MQ-1_Djibouti_ExecSum_21%20Feb%2012.pdf, (predator Drone started losing oil and the engine eventually stopped which resulted in a crash).

[42] *See Mq-1b Predator Accident Report Released*, AIR COMBAT COMMAND (Jan. 1, 2013), http://www.acc.af.mil/news/story.asp?id=123332108, (pilot error along with the predator drone losing both alternators caused the crash).

[43] *See MQ-1B Predator accident report released*, AIR COMBAT COMMAND (April 9, 2013), http://www.acc.af.mil/news/story.asp?id=123343632, ("[R]emotely piloted aircraft satellite data link disconnected. The mishap pilot ran the appropriate checklist, but was unsuccessful in reestablishing a satellite link. The mishap remotely piloted aircraft impacted approximately 3.25 nautical miles south-southwest of the point where the link was lost.").

[44] *See* David Cenciotti, *Video Of Drone Crashing Into Cargo Plane In Afghanistan Raises Concern Over German UAV Safety*, BUSINESS INSIDER (Jul. 16, 2013 7:13 AM), http://www.businessinsider.com/drone-crash-raises-concern-over-safety-2013-7, (German UA accidentally started up by pilot and then almost runs over two people and crashes into a parked cargo plane in Afghanistan.)

[45] *See* John Reed, *Midair Collision Between a C-130 and a UAV*, DEFENSETECH (Aug. 17, 2011), http://defensetech.org/2011/08/17/midair-collision-between-a-c-130-and-a-uav/, (UA and C-130 crashed into each other).

people?[46] All of those questions should make one wonder at the many difficult problems that need to be solved before one can integrate unmanned airplanes into the U.S. airspace. On top of the problems with fully integrating the UA into U.S. airspace, other countries are working to integrate UA within their own airspace. This adds another level of problems that now arises because of the need for standardization of UA for flying or selling internationally.

---

[46] *See* Geoffrey Ingersoll, *Frightening Drone Footage Shows Near Miss With Airbus A300 Over Kabul*, BUSINESS INSIDER (June 3, 2013 3:33PM), http://www.businessinsider.com/drone-video-near-miss-over-kabul-2013-6, (German UA missed passenger jet by less than 50 ft.).

CHAPTER THREE: THE UNITED STATES AIRSPACE AND THE LAWS GOVERNING

This section is going to talk about the laws that give the FAA authority to regulate the United States' airspace, the dimensions of that airspace, and how that airspace interacts with the terrestrial property rights of land owners on the ground. Next, this section will discuss how the FAA educates and regulates using different types of FAA documents and then take a more in-depth look at the specific FAA documents that have been created pertaining to UA operations.

A. THE AUTHORITY FOR THE FAA'S REGULATION OF NAVIGABLE AIRSPACE

The Commerce Clause of the U.S. Constitution gives Congress authority to "regulate commerce with foreign nations, and among the several states."[47] Congress created the Federal Aviation Agency by the Federal Aviation Act of 1958,[48] but in 1967, Congress changed the name into the Federal Aviation Administration ("FAA") and moved that agency into the Department of Transportation ("DOT") which is a Presidential cabinet department.[49] The FAA has been given by Congress jurisdiction to regulate navigable airspace of aircraft by regulation or order.[50]

B. NAVIGABLE AIRSPACE

Navigable airspace is under the regulation of the FAA, but what are the boundaries of navigable airspace? Are there different types of navigable airspace? How far down does navigable airspace go? This section aims to deal with these questions.

---

[47] U.S CONST. art. I, § 8; *see also* 49 U.S.C. § 40103 (a)(1)("The United States Government has exclusive sovereignty of airspace of the United States.").

[48] Federal Aviation Act, Pub. L. No. 85-726, 72 Stat. 731 (1958).

[49] *See A Brief History of the FAA*, FED. AVIATION ADMIN., http://www.faa.gov/about/history/brief_history/

[50] *See* 49 U.S.C. § 40103(b)(1)(Congress delegated to the FAA the job to "develop plans and policy for the use of the *navigable airspace* and assign by *regulation or order* the use of the airspace necessary to ensure the safety of *aircraft* and the efficient use of airspace.")(emphasis mine).

1. The Black and White Areas of Navigable Airspace

"'[N]avigable airspace' means airspace above the minimum altitudes of flight prescribed by regulations."[51] Navigable airspace was further defined in the Federal Aviation Regulations ("FARs") as "airspace at and above the minimum flight altitudes prescribed by or under this chapter, including airspace needed for safe takeoff and landing."[52] In chapter 91 of the FARs, minimum flight altitudes for airplanes are defined as 1,000 feet above the highest obstacle and 2,000 feet horizontally from the highest obstacle in the "congested area of a city, town, or settlement, or over open air assembly of persons."[53] The airplane can, in uncongested areas, operate at an altitude of 500 feet above the ground or even lower when over water or sparsely populated areas where the airplane only has to be operated over and around a 500 feet bubble from "any person, vessel, vehicle, or structure"[54] providing that if the airplane's engine fails that a hazard

---

[51] 49 U.S.C. § 40102(32).
[52] 14 C.F.R. § 1.1.
[53] 14 C.F.R. § 91.119(b).
[54] 14 C.F.R. § 91.119(c).

will not be created to person or property on the surface.[55] The only

exception for airplanes to fly below these altitudes is "when necessary

for takeoff or landing"[56] or when necessary to meet an emergency.[57]

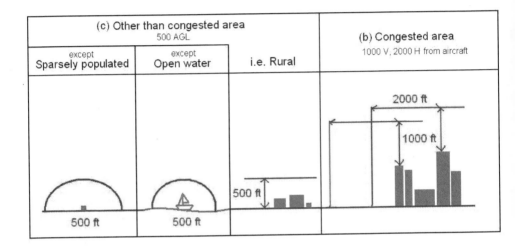

Figure of § 91.119[58]

Helicopters can be operated below the altitudes just discussed so

long as an engine failure will not cause a hazard,[59] but how low a

helicopter pilot can fly is really limited by the rule that "[n]o person

---

[55] 14 C.F.R. § 91.119(a).

[56] *Id.*

[57] *See* 14 C.F.R. § 91.3(b).

[58] http://www.hostpic.org/images/3191.119.jpg. (last visited Jan. 21, 2015) (used with author's permission).

[59] 14 C.F.R. § 91.119(d).

may operate an aircraft in a careless or reckless manner so as to endanger the life or property of another."[60]

2. TERRESTRIAL PROPERTY RIGHTS INTERACTING WITH NAVIGABLE AIRSPACE

United States v. Causby[61] gives a clue as to where private property rights of airspace end and navigable airspace *could* start. In *Causby*, the context was that World War II was taking place, and a farmer had a farm with chickens.[62] This farm was located right near an airport that had large military aircraft flying in and out, as low as 83 feet above his farm and 18 feet above the highest tree, which resulted in the chickens dying from flying into the walls from being scared.[63]

The farmer sued, and the Court held that Congress declared the airspace above what was deemed the minimum safe altitude ("MSA") to be in the public domain and that whatever was above the MSA was immune from any suits against the government for a takings violation.[64] The Court went on to talk about airspace below the MSA

---

[60] 14 C.F.R. § 91.13, ("Careless or reckless operation").
[61] 328 U.S. 256 (1946).
[62] *Id.* at 258.
[63] *Id.* at 258-59.
[64] *Id.* at 263-64.

and held that people's property ends at the highest of the underlying land's trees, buildings, fences,[65] "immediate reaches of the enveloping atmosphere[,]"[66] or how high the owner can "occupy or use [the airspace] in connection with the land[.]"[67] The lowest navigable airspace could ever be argued to descend to is just over this unless the "airspace [is] needed for landing or taking off."[68] The Court found in favor of the farmer and declared that there was a Fifth Amendment taking requiring just compensation because the flights over the farmer's field were "so low and so frequent as to be a direct and immediate interference with the enjoyment and use of the land" but the Court declined to define where the precise boundaries of public airspace above the farm meet the immediate reaches of the farmer's property. [69]Many other cases have followed *Causby*.[70]

---

[65] *Id.* at 264.
[66] *Id.*
[67] *Id.*
[68] *Id.* at 265.
[69] *See U.S. v Causby*, 328 U.S. 256, 266 (1946).
[70] *See* Alissa Dolan & Richard Thompson II, CONG. RESEARCH SERV., R42940, *Integration of Drones into Domestic Airspace: Selected Legal Issues 8 (2013)*, *available at* http://www.fas.org/sgp/crs/natsec/R42940.pdf (mentioning that the post-*Causby* cases resolving property issues involving airspace use *Causby* as a starting point but then break off into one of three lines of theory in resolving the cases.).

Another issue here is how high do states and local governments rights extend up to? States have the general police power, but what happens if they start requiring their state-specific drone licenses or all together ban drones? The lack of clear regulation in this area can cause havoc. Imagine trying to fly your drone and every county or city has its own drone laws. For a brief discussion in this area read McKenna, Long, & Aldridge's petition for preemption.[71]

3. Is There a Gray Area? Does Uncontrolled Airspace Mean Unregulated Airspace?

From this "Causby bubble," to 400 feet[72] is what the focus of this next section will be. This area is class G airspace and class G is considered uncontrolled airspace which means that air traffic control "has no authority or responsibility to control air traffic[.]"[73] Air traffic

---

[71] Mark A. Dombroff and Lawrence S. Ebner petition to Michael Huerta (Oct. 10, 2014), https://www.mckennalong.com/assets/attachments/PreemptionLetterFAA.pdf

[72] *See* 14 C.F.R. § 91.119(d); *see also Florida v. Riley*, 488 U.S. 445, 451 (1989)("Any member of the public could legally have been flying over Riley's property in a helicopter at the altitude of 400 feet and could have observed Riley's greenhouse.").

[73] Pilot's Handbook of Aeronautical Knowledge, Fed. Aviation. Admin., at 14-3, *available at* https://www.faa.gov/regulations_policies/handbooks_manuals/aviation/pilot_handbook/media/PHAK%20-%20Chapter%2014.pdf

control does not have authority but does the FAA have authority to control air traffic?

This area has become a big issue for some[74] advocating that the FAA does not have jurisdiction below 400 feet. Generally, the argument against FAA jurisdiction over this area is that Congress gave the FAA the power to regulate navigable airspace[75] and to define[76] it, the FAA has defined navigable airspace in 14 C.F.R. § 91.119, limiting its jurisdiction, but the FAA is now seeking to exercise authority below 400 feet with regards to UA. The black and white of the FAA's navigable airspace jurisdiction begins at 400 feet above ground level for helicopters[77] and 500 feet for airplanes,[78] unless the aircraft is taking off, landing, or having an emergency. This area

---

[74] See Pirker's Motion to Dismiss, *infra* note 350, at 10; *see also*, Peter Sachs, *Busting the FAA's "Myth Busting" Document*, http://dronelawjournal.com/busting-the-faas-myth-busting-document/.

[75] See 49 U.S.C. § 40103(b)(1).

[76] See 49 U.S.C. § 40102(32).

[77] See 14 C.F.R. § 91.119(d); *see also Florida v. Riley*, 488 U.S. 445, 451 (1989)("Any member of the public could legally have been flying over Riley's property in a helicopter at the altitude of 400 feet and could have observed Riley's greenhouse.").

[78] Many courts have held that 500 feet is the floor of navigable airspace. *See Persyn v. United States*, 34 Fed. Cl. 187 (Fed. Cl. 1995) *aff'd*, 106 F.3d 424 (Fed. Cir. 1996); *Powell v. United States*, 1 Cl. Ct. 669 (Cl. Ct. 1983); *A. J. Hodges Indus., Inc. v. United States*, 355 F.2d 592, 594 (Ct. Cl. 1966).

below navigable airspace is a "gray" jurisdictional area for them to try and regulate.

The FAA can counter by arguing that airspace below 400 feet can be regulated even though 49 U.S.C. § 40103(b)(1) specifically says "navigable airspace" because 49 U.S.C. § 44701(a) does not have a navigable airspace limitation and says:

> **(a) Promoting Safety.**—The Administrator of the Federal Aviation Administration shall promote safe flight of civil aircraft in air commerce by prescribing—
>
> **(1)** minimum standards required in the interest of safety for appliances and for the design, material, construction, quality of work, and performance of aircraft, aircraft engines, and propellers;
>
> **(2)** regulations and minimum standards in the interest of safety for—
>
>> **(A)** inspecting, servicing, and overhauling aircraft, aircraft engines, propellers, and appliances;
>>
>> **(B)** equipment and facilities for, and the timing and manner of, the inspecting, servicing, and overhauling; and
>>
>> **(C)** a qualified private person, instead of an officer or employee of the Administration, to examine and report on the inspecting, servicing, and overhauling;
>
> **(3)** regulations required in the interest of safety for the reserve supply of aircraft, aircraft engines, propellers, appliances, and aircraft fuel and oil, including the reserve supply of fuel and oil carried in flight;
>
> **(4)** regulations in the interest of safety for the maximum hours or periods of service of airmen and other employees of air carriers; and

(5) regulations and minimum standards for other practices, methods, and procedure the Administrator finds necessary for safety in air commerce and national security.

This is why the FAA has regulatory jurisdiction over motorized paragliders,[79] moored balloons and kites,[80] amateur rockets,[81] large cranes or building construction near an airport,[82] mechanics working on registered aircraft on the ground,[83] pilots taxiing aircraft on the ground,[84] and many more things that are all below 400 feet.

Furthermore, the FAA could also say that in the FAA Modernization and Reform Act of 2012, Congress limited the FAA's authority to promulgate regulations pertaining to model aircraft; however, "Nothing in [that] section shall be construed to limit the authority of the [FAA] to pursue enforcement action against persons

---

[79] *See* 14 C.F.R. § 103; *see also* FAA Legal Interpretation to Barbara Parisi from Rebecca MacPherson, Acting Assistant Chief Counsel (April 2, 2006), *available at* http://www.faa.gov/about/office_org/headquarters_offices/agc/pol_adjudication/agc_200/interpretations/data/interps/2006/parisi-uscpsc%20-%20(2006)%20legal%20interpretation.pdf

[80] 14 C.F.R. §§ 101.11-19.

[81] 14 C.F.R. §§ 101.21-29.

[82] 14 C.F.R. § 77.9(b).

[83] *See* 14 C.F.R. § 43.1; *see also* Borregard v. Nat'l Transp. Safety Bd., 46 F.3d 944, 945 (9th Cir. 1995);
FAA Legal Interpretation to Craig Easter from Rebecca MacPherson, Acting Assistant Chief Counsel (Aug. 6, 2010), *available at* http://www.faa.gov/about/office_org/headquarters_offices/agc/pol_adjudication/agc_200/interpretations/data/interps/2010/easter%20-%20(2010)%20legal%20interpretation.pdf

[84] *Miranda v. Nat'l Transp. Safety Bd.*, 866 F.2d 805(5th Cir. 1989); *Borden v. Adm'r of F.A.A.*, 849 F.2d 319, 320 (8th Cir. 1988).

operating model aircraft who endanger the safety of the national airspace system."[85] The FAA did not say navigable airspace but *national* airspace system.

The key to why the FAA can regulate below navigable airspace is that there are regulations in place that specifically regulate those things. Are there regulations for UA that operate below 400 feet? Keep reading to find out.

4. THE DIFFERENT TYPES OF NAVIGABLE AIRSPACE

It is helpful to briefly discuss the different types of navigable airspace. Airspace is classified based upon altitude and width with each particular type of airspace having certain visibility, cloud clearance, aircraft speed, and pilot requirements. The different types of airspace are class A, B, C, D, E, and G.[86] The way I taught my flight students to quickly remember the different airspace classes was A for altitude, B for busy, C for congested, D for a "dorky wanabe" class C airport, E for everywhere, and G for ground. Class A has the most

---

[85] FMRA § 336(b), *infra* note 233; 126 STAT. 77.
[86] The FAA has not created Class F airspace.

requirements while G the least. Class B, C, and D are located around

airports.

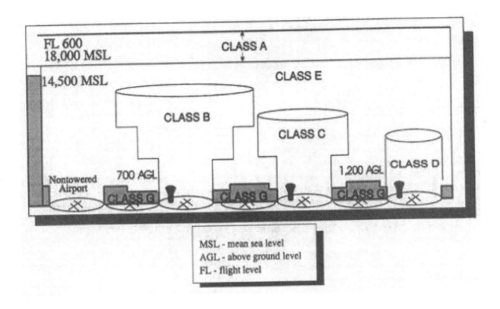

The Different Types of Airspace[87]

C. HOW THE FAA REGULATES NAVIGABLE AIRSPACE

The FAA controls the airspace by regulations and orders. The

FAA has created regulations,[88] known as the Federal Aviation

Regulations ("FARs"), which govern the certification of only civil

---

[87] FED. AVIATION ADMIN., *Airmen's Information Manual*, FIG 3-2-1, *available at* https://www.faa.gov/air_traffic/publications/atpubs/aim/aim0302.html

[88] 14 C.F.R. §§ 1-199.

aircraft,[89] civil pilot licensing,[90] airspace,[91] commercial operations,[92] general pilot operating rules,[93] pilot schools and certificated agencies,[94] airports,[95] and navigational facilities.[96]

In the FARs, the terms UA, RPA, unmanned, or anything else coming close to those terms are not being used in any of the rules. However, the definitions of aircraft in 49 U.S.C. § 40102(6), "any contrivance invented, used, or designed to navigate, or fly in, the air[]"[97] and in 14 C.F.R. § 1.1, "a device that is used or intended to be used for flight in the air[,]"[98] are both broad enough so as to encompass UA without explicitly defining them. It can be argued that the broadness is a problem because even paper airplanes, bullets, Frisbees, baseballs, footballs, and balloons would fall into those definitions. When reading the FARs, however, one must pay particular attention to the context in which the word aircraft is being used to see

---

[89] 14 C.F.R. §§ 21-49.
[90] 14 C.F.R. §§ 61-67.
[91] 14 C.F.R. §§ 71-77.
[92] 14 C.F.R. §§ 119-135.
[93] 14 C.F.R. §§ 91-105.
[94] 14 C.F.R. §§ 141-147.
[95] 14 C.F.R. §§ 150-161.
[96] 14 C.F.R. §§ 170-171.
[97] 49 U.S.C. § 40102(6).
[98] 14 C.F.R. § 1.1.

if the regulation is applicable because at the beginning of 14 C.F.R. § 1.1 the definitions also says, "unless the context requires otherwise[.]"[99] One interesting thing to note is that 14 C.F.R. § 91.1(c) says, "This part applies to each person on board an aircraft being operated under this part, unless otherwise specified[,]" and this seems to indicate contextually that part 91 operations might not apply to persons operating the aircraft remotely.

Aircraft does not mean all aircraft all the time. There are certain modifiers for the term "aircraft" such as civil aircraft, model aircraft, and public aircraft, which more specifically define the aircraft term being talked about. The FAA treats each of these aircraft differently.

1. HOW THE FAA CREATES NEW REGULATIONS

The FAA's regulation making process is governed by administrative rules created by the Administrative Procedures Act,[100] the Federal Register rules,[101] and the FAA's own rules.[102]

---

[99] *Id.*
[100] 5 U.S.C. § 553.
[101] 44 U.S.C. §§ 1501-1511.
[102] 14 C.F.R. 11.1.

Generally,[103] when the FAA wants to create a regulation, they can publish an Advanced Notice of Proposed Rule Making[104] ("ANRPM") or Notice of Proposed Rule Making[105] ("NPRM") in the Federal Register,[106] unless the FAA has good cause[107] to issue regulation such as in an emergency. The NPRM will receive comments from the general public,[108] hence the reason why the process is called "notice and comment." Once the FAA has taken into account the comments, the FAA would again publish in the Federal Register what the final rule[109] will be that will take effect in no less than 30 days.[110] These regulations are binding and have the force of law.

---

[103] There are some exceptions to this process but this is how it generally happens.

[104] 14 C.F.R. § 11.3 ("(ANPRM) tells the public that FAA is considering an area for rulemaking and requests written comments on the appropriate scope of the rulemaking or on specific topics. An advance notice of proposed rulemaking may or may not include the text of potential changes to a regulation.").

[105] 14 C.F.R. § 11.5 ("A notice of proposed rulemaking (NPRM) proposes FAA's specific regulatory changes for public comment and contains supporting information. It includes proposed regulatory text.").

[106] See 5 U.S.C. § 553(b).

[107] Id. § 553(b)(3)(B) ("[W]hen the agency for good cause finds . . . that notice and public procedure thereon are impracticable, unnecessary, or contrary to the public interest."); 14 C.F.R. § 11.29.

[108] See id. § 553(c).

[109] See 14 C.F.R. § 11.9 ("A final rule sets out new or revised requirements and their effective date.").

[110] 5 U.S.C. § 553(c)-(d).

2. THE FAA CAN CHOOSE TO GRANT EXEMPTIONS TO THE REGULATIONS

"The Administrator of the Federal Aviation Administration may grant an exemption from a regulation prescribed" [111] under § 40103(b)(2) which says:

> The Administrator shall prescribe air traffic regulations on the flight of aircraft (including regulations on safe altitudes) for—
>
> (A) navigating, protecting, and identifying aircraft;
>
> (B) protecting individuals and property on the ground;
>
> (C) using the navigable airspace efficiently; and
>
> (D) preventing collision between aircraft, between aircraft and land or water vehicles, and between aircraft and airborne objects.[112]

The regulations on how to go about requesting the exemption are located in 14 C.F.R. §§ 11.15, 11.63, and 11.81. An operator might try the exemption approach if they want to operate their aircraft but the regulation they want relief from is not listed as available for a certificate of waiver in 14 C.F.R. § 91.905. Additionally, anyone going the exemption route as opposed to obtaining a special airworthiness certificate (SAC) should keep in mind that the exemption will be published in the Federal Register and receive

---

[111] 49 U.S.C. § 40109.
[112] 49 U.S.C. § 40103(b)(2)(A)-(D).

comments while the SAC route is a "less public" route of obtaining operational approval.[113]

The FAA has granted exemptions to manned aircraft such as in the example of Boeing being granted the exemption from 14 C.F.R. §§ 25.841(a)(2)-(a)(3), cabin depressurization requirements, which otherwise, would not have allowed the Boeing 787 from being certified for high altitude operation. [114] Many other notable exemptions include the FAA granting the "DoD exemptions from 14 CFR 91.209 (Night Vision Goggle (NVG) lights out training in Military Operating Areas (MOAs)), 14 CFR 91.81 (altimeter settings in MOAs and restricted areas), 14 CFR 105.17 and 105.19 (unlighted night parachute operations), 14 CFR 91.117, 91.159, and 91.209 (speed, VFR cruising altitudes, and aircraft lighting for drug interdictions), and 14 CFR 91.119 (IFR operations along all-weather low-altitude routes)[.]"[115]

---

[113] *See* 14 C.F.R. § 11.81(f).
[114] *See* Petition from Boeing Co., to U.S. Dep't of Transp., Petition for Exemption from FAR §§ 25.841(a)(2) and (a)(3) with Respect to Uncontained Engine Failures, Docket No. FAA-2004-19890 (Dec. 10, 2004), *available at* www.regulations.gov#!documentDetail;D=FAA-2004-19890-0001
[115] LESTER, ET AL., USAF AIRBORNE SENSE AND AVOID (ABSAA) AIRWORTHINESS AND OPERATIONAL APPROVAL APPROACH 19, *available at*

As a taste of things to come, published in the Federal Register in 2013 was a petition[116] from Isiscopter for exemption[117] "relief to operate small unmanned aircraft systems within visual line of sight of the pilot in command for commercial purposes."[118] The FAA did not respond to the exemption petition within the deadline.

Currently, individuals are petitioning under section 333 of the FAA Modernization and Reform Act, discussed later, to have their aircraft as well as themselves be exempted from the regulations because manned aircraft regulations are extremely burdensome to comply with for unmanned aircraft. A Section 333 petition is the mechanism to obtain relief from burdensome regulations and is not an airworthiness certificate. It is an ad-hoc fix. The regulations that a person or company would need relief from are beyond the scope of this book.

---

http://www.mitre.org/sites/default/files/publications/usaf-airborne-sense-avoid-13-3116.pdf.

[116] See Petition for Exemption, 78 Fed. Reg. 3,068 (proposed Feb. 4, 2013), available at http://www.gpo.gov/fdsys/pkg/FR-2013-01-15/pdf/2013-00625.pdf

[117] See 14 C.F.R. § 11.15 ("A petition for exemption is a request to FAA by an individual or entity asking for relief from the requirements of a current regulation.").

[118] See Petition for Exemption, supra note 116.

3. TYPES OF FAA DOCUMENTS

The FAA also publishes documents in addition to the regulations to help educate the public. There are two types of documents that this book will be discussing, Advisory Circulars and Policy Statements.

Advisory Circulars ("AC") are just that, advisory. AC's are not binding, unless the AC is incorporated specifically by reference into a regulation.[119] "An AC is issued to provide guidance and information in a designated subject area or to show a method acceptable to the Administrator for complying with a related Federal Aviation Regulation."[120] The FAA issues AC in a systematic way. AC "are issued in a numbered-subject system corresponding to the subject areas of the Federal Aviation Regulations (FAR's)"[121] Each AC "has a subject number either followed by a dash and a consecutive number (135-15) or a period with a specific FAR section number, followed by a dash and a consecutive number (135.169-2) identifying the

---

[119] *See* FED. AVIATION ADMIN., Advisory Circular 00-2.11, Advisory Circular Checklist and Status of Other FAA Publications 1 (1997), *available at* http://ntl.bts.gov/lib/000/200/208/ac00-2.11.pdf, ("Unless incorporated into a regulation by reference, the contents of an advisory circular are not binding on the public.").
[120] *Id.* at i.
[121] *Id.*

individual circular."[122] Example: AC **91**-57 deals with all of Part **91** while AC **35.16**-1 deals with **Section 35.16**, not all of Part 35. The number following the dash "is not used again in the same subject series. Revised circulars have a letter A, B, C, etc."[123] Example: AC 65-32A is not the first but *second* edition.

The FAA also publishes policy statements and guidance material. Policy statements "merely represent[] an agency position with respect to how it will treat—typically enforce—the governing legal norm. By issuing a policy statement, an agency simply lets the public know its current enforcement or adjudicatory approach. The agency retains the discretion and the authority to change its position—even abruptly—in any specific case because a change in its policy does not affect the legal norm."[124] Simply put, the policy statements will be "explanatory rather than mandatory."[125]

---

[122] *Id.* at A2-4.
[123] *Id.*
[124] *Syncor Int'l.. Corp. v. Shalala*, 127 F.3d 90, 94 (D.C. Cir. 1997).
[125] DOUGLAS M. MARSHALL, *U.S. Aviation Regulatory System*, *in* INTRODUCTION TO UNMANNED AIRCRAFT SYSTEMS 40 (Barnhart et al. eds., 2012).

4. ADVISORY CIRCULARS PERTAINING TO UNMANNED AIRCRAFT

The AC that applies to the discussion of UA is AC 91-57, which was issued in 1981 to *encourage model aircraft flyers* to *voluntarily* comply with the safety standards in the circular.[126] It is a one page circular that encourages the modelers to operate their aircraft: not in the presence of spectators unless the airplane has been flight tested, not more than 400 feet above the ground, not within 3 miles of an airport unless notifying the control tower or flight service station, not near noise-sensitive areas, and not over populated areas. [127] Interestingly, AC 91-57 was accidentally cancelled for a short period of time.[128] This AC will be phased out sometime in the future.

5. POLICY STATEMENTS, ORDERS, AND GUIDANCE PERTAINING TO UNMANNED AIRCRAFT

This section is where much of the confusion over UA comes from. This area is difficult to understand because the area is *constantly*

---

[126] *See* FED. AVIATION ADMIN., Advisory Circular 91-57, Model Aircraft Operating Standards 1 (1981) [hereinafter "AC 91-57"], *available at* http://www.faa.gov/documentLibrary/media/Advisory_Circular/91-57.pdf

[127] *See id.*

[128] *See* Press, *AC 91-57 Cancelled in Error*, sUAS NEWS, (Oct. 14, 2014) http://www.suasnews.com/2014/10/31829/ac-91-57-cancelled-in-error/

40

evolving. Compounding that problem is the FAA not updating its webpages to cite the current policy statements[129] or the FAA not noting in their database that a document has been updated so as to alert someone searching for the current document.[130] On top of all of that, the FAA has been repeatedly updating its "myth busting page"[131] and "myth busting page- update"[132] which is causing even more confusion among individuals.[133] The author has created links monitoring both of the myth busting pages for additions or subtractions that the FAA

---

[129] *See Unmanned Aircraft Systems (UAS) Regulations & Policies*, FED. AVIATION ADMIN, http://www.faa.gov/about/initiatives/uas/reg/ (where as of April 11, 2014, N 8900.207 is listed as a reference even though it was canceled July 30, 2013 by N8900.227).

[130] *Compare* Document Information for 8130.34B, FED. AVIATION ADMIN http://www.faa.gov/regulations_policies/orders_notices/index.cfm/go/document.information/documentID/1019693 (not showing that 8130.34B is canceled but showing that 8130.34B cancels 8130.34A) *with* Document Information for 8130.34C, FED. AVIATION ADMIN, http://www.faa.gov/regulations_policies/orders_notices/index.cfm/go/document.information/documentID/1021706 (which does not say that it canceled 8130.34B).

[131] *Busting Myths about the FAA and Unmanned Aircraft*, FED. AVIATION ADMIN, http://www.faa.gov/news/updates/?newsId=76240

[132] *Busting Myths about the FAA and Unmanned Aircraft–Update*, FED. AVIATION ADMIN, http://www.faa.gov/news/updates/?newsId=76381

[133] For example, after the FAA lost in the NTSB ruling, talked about later in this book, which came out on March 6, 2013, the FAA on March 8 updated the document from the original "but hobbyists must operate according to" to "However, hobbyist are advised to operate their aircraft in accordance with . . . ." Individuals should definitely sign up at www.changedetection.com for the mythbusting page to keep track of the additions as well as the subtractions the FAA does to the page.

does.[134] This is not to criticize the FAA but to make readers aware of the *constantly evolving* nature of this area.

It must also be noted that the discussions of the policy statements below are not to be a substitute for reading the policy statements themselves. The policy statements will not be analyzed *exhaustively* below but the important and interesting areas will be analyzed. It must be stressed that individuals interested in working in this area should seek legal counsel.

The FAA policy statements have been one of the main areas that critics[135] of the FAA have focused on. One critic[136] in his analysis of the FAA, quoted a case involving the Environmental Protection Agency ("EPA") which effectively summarized what the critic felt was the problem with the FAA's policy statements.

---

[134] For the Myth Busting Page, https://www.changedetection.com/log/gov/faa/updates_log4.html, and for the Myth Busting Update page, https://www.changedetection.com/log/gov/faa/updates_log3.html?emsg=1001. Changes for the original page only go back to April 26, 2014 but another individual has been tracking that page for longer. https://www.changedetection.com/log/gov/faa/updates_log2.html#changelist

[135] *See*, e.g., John Frank Weaver, *Maybe the FAA Doesn't Have the Authority to Regulate Unmanned Aerial Vehicles*, SUAS NEWS (Mar. 5, 2014), http://www.suasnews.com/2014/03/27899/maybe-the-faa-doesnt-have-the-authority-to-regulate-unmanned-aerial-vehicles/

[136] *See id.*

42

The phenomenon we see in this case is familiar. Congress passes a broadly worded statute. The agency follows with regulations containing broad language, open-ended phrases, ambiguous standards and the like. Then as years pass, the agency issues circulars or guidance or memoranda, explaining, interpreting, defining and often expanding the commands in the regulations. One guidance document may yield another and then another and so on. Several words in a regulation may spawn hundreds of pages of text as the agency offers more and more detail regarding what its regulations demand of regulated entities. Law is made, without notice and comment, without public participation, and without publication in the Federal Register or the Code of Federal Regulations. With the advent of the Internet, the agency does not need these official publications to ensure widespread circulation; it can inform those affected simply by posting its new guidance or memoranda or policy statement on its web site. An agency operating in this way gains a large advantage. 'It can issue or amend its real rules, i.e., its interpretative rules and policy statements, quickly and inexpensively without following any statutorily prescribed procedures.'. . . The agency may also think there is another advantage—immunizing its lawmaking from judicial review.[137]

The FAA would respond, "The United States has the busiest, most complex airspace in the world, including many general aviation aircraft that we must consider when planning UAS integration, because those same airplanes and small UAS may occupy the same

---

[137] *Appalachian Power Co. v. E.P.A.*, 208 F.3d 1015, 1020 (D.C. Cir. 2000).

airspace[,]"[138] and with technology rapidly changing, this creates a quick moving target that the FAA has to hit with the first shot.

Finally, some of the documents talked about in this section are notices or orders. "An Order/Notice is a directive that the FAA uses to issue policy, instructions and work information to its own personnel and designees. It spells out how the FAA expects to carry out its responsibilities."[139] The difference between the two is that notices normally end at a certain time while orders continue on.

a. THE 2005 POLICY STATEMENT

The first policy statement that the FAA published that pertains to UA was Unmanned Aircraft Systems Operations in the U.S. National Airspace System – Interim Operational Approval Guidance and was published in September 2005 ("2005 policy").[140] The purpose of the policy statement was to "develop guidance for Federal Aviation

---

[138] *Supra*, note 132.

[139] *Orders/Notices*, FED. AVIATION ADMIN., http://rgl.faa.gov/Regulatory_and_Guidance_Library/rgOrders.nsf/MainFrame?Open Frameset

[140] FED. AVIATION ADMIN., AFS-400 UAS Policy 05-01, UNMANNED AIRCRAFT SYSTEMS OPERATIONS IN THE U.S. NATIONAL AIRSPACE SYSTEM—INTERIM OPERATIONAL APPROVAL GUIDANCE 1 (2005) [hereinafter "2005 Policy Statement"], *available at* http://www.uavm.com/images/AFS-400_05-01_faa_uas_policy.pdf

Administration organizations to use when evaluating applications for

Certificate(s) of Waiver or Authorization.[("COA")] This policy is not

meant as a substitute for any regulatory process."[141] The statement

further went on to clarify how public aircraft[142] operators could

receive a COA while civil aircraft operators could not apply for a

COA but would have to apply for a special airworthiness certificate in

the experimental[143] category ("SAC-EC").[144] The statement lists many

different ways UA can be flown but the most applicable to this book is

flights below 18,000ft and not on an instrument flight rules ("IFR")

flight plan which will have to be conducted within line of sight

("LOS") of the observer within 1 mile laterally and no more than

3,000 feet vertically.[145] Furthermore, the public aircraft operator

applicant would have to show that the aircraft is "airworthy." There

must be a pilot and an observer who are to have at least third class

medicals,[146] while the pilot is additionally to have passed the private

---

[141] *Id.* at 1.
[142] Public vs. civil aircraft will be discussed later in the book.
[143] *See* 14 C.F.R. § 21.191.
[144] *See* 2005 Policy Statement, *supra* note140, at 4.
[145] *See id.* at 5.
[146] *See id.* at 3.

pilot knowledge exam.[147] This policy statement caused problems because it said:

> **Model Aircraft.** Advisory Circular (AC) 91-57, Model Aircraft Operating Standards, published in 1981, applies to model aircraft. UA that comply with the guidance in AC 91-57 are considered model aircraft and are not evaluated by the UA criteria in this policy.[148]

Thus, since it is far easier to operate as a model aircraft under AC 91-57 instead of trying to obtain a COA or a SAC-EC, many people tried to operate only under AC 91-57.

b. THE 2007 POLICY STATEMENT

In February 2007, the FAA published a notice of policy[149] ("2007 Notice") in the Federal Register to clarify the "FAA's current policy concerning operations of unmanned aircraft in the National Airspace System."[150] The FAA answered the problem created by the 2005 policy statement's AC 91-57 "loophole," saying: "[t]he FAA recognizes that people and companies other than modelers might be

---

[147] *See id.* at 7.

[148] *See id.* at 6.

[149] *See* Notice of Unmanned Aircraft Operations in the National Airspace System Policy, 72 Fed. Reg. 6,689 (proposed Feb. 13, 2007) [hereinafter the "2007 Notice"], *available at* https://www.faa.gov/about/office_org/headquarters_offices/ato/service_units/system ops/aaim/organizations/uas/coa/faq/media/frnotice_uas.pdf

[150] *Id.*

flying UAS with the mistaken understanding that they are legally operating under the authority of AC 91-57. AC 91-57 only applies to modelers, and thus specifically excludes its use by persons or companies for business purposes."[151]

This policy statement gives the same definition of unmanned aircraft as the 2005 Policy as "a device that is used, or is intended to be used, for flight in the air with no onboard pilot[,]"[152] and this 2007 Notice goes on to say that "[r]egulatory standards need to be developed to enable current technology for unmanned aircraft to comply with Title 14 Code of Federal Regulations ("CFR")."[153]

The policy statement declares that "the current FAA policy for UAS operations is that no person may operate a UAS in the National Airspace System without specific authority"[154] but it does not cite any authority, statutes, or cases, that specific authority is needed to operate a UA. Critics of the FAA would say that this policy requirement was pulled out of "thin air."

---

[151] 2007 Notice, *supra* note 149, at 6,690.
[152] *Id.*
[153] *Id.*
[154] *Id.* at 5.

The policy statement goes on to say civil aircraft operate under the authority of a special airworthiness certificate in the experimental category ("SAC-EC"), public aircraft operate under the authority of a COA, and model aircraft operate under the authority of AC 91-57.[155] This raises the interesting question of how can AC-91-57 be used as an authority when AC 91-57 says nothing about granting authority for model aircraft operations, and to construe it as providing such authority is completely unfaithful to its text and its express intent of encouraging voluntary compliance with recommended safety guidelines.

In regulation 14 C.F.R § 91.319, SAC-EC aircraft are prohibited from "[c]arrying persons or property for compensation or hire[,]"[156] but remarkably this notice of policy changed the limitations placed on the SAC-EC UA to being more restrictive. Regulation 91.319 says, "no carrying person or property for compensation or hire" but the 2007 Notice says just "no compensation or hire." This change makes sense in the FAA's eyes because some UA operators taking photographs would just argue that they are not *carrying* persons or

---

[155] *See id.*
[156] 14 C.F.R. § 91.319(a)(2).

property but just gathering data and storing that data onboard in a digital format. The FAA explains that AC 91-57 applies to modelers who fly their aircraft as a "hobby or for recreational use"[157] even though there has never been a distinction of model flying for business or recreation in any policy statements or regulations.

The two big problems created now are that (1) SAC-EC aircraft cannot operate for compensation or hire at all, and (2) model aircraft cannot be operated for business because model aircraft are only recreational. This policy statement creates the term "business purposes" but does not define this term in the policy or in any of the regulations. The term "business purposes" cannot be analogized to "commercial operations" or used interchangeably even though that is being done by the FAA.[158] The term "business purposes" is *nowhere* defined, while the term "commercial operator" is defined as "a person who, for compensation or hire, engages in the carriage by aircraft in

---

[157] 2007 Notice, *supra* note 149, at 6690.
[158] *Busting Myths about the FAA and Unmanned Aircraft*, FED. AVIATION ADMIN., http://www.faa.gov/news/updates/?newsId=76240 (The FAA used the term "commercial operations" when answering the "myths" about unmanned aircraft.).

air commerce of persons or property, other than as an air carrier or foreign air carrier or under the authority of Part 375 of this title."[159]

The term "business purposes," as the FAA used it in the 2007 Notice, can be somewhat figured out by looking at how the FAA has handled the Drone Prize 2014 contest where $10,000 of prizes will be given away to people who videotaped their UA flying for a civic purpose to improve society.[160] A contest with a prize is different than commercial operations because with a contest there is no certainty that you will be paid. This begs further questions. When does the hobbyist turn into a commercial UA pilot? What if a farmer organized a contest to whoever could take the best pictures of his farm? Better yet, what if a university put out a contest to whoever could take the best pictures of the university?

If one could analogize a person flying a UA for compensation, "business purposes," as a commercial operator, and assuming that just for the sake of discussion, what type of commercial operation is a UA flying for aerial photography when aerial photography has been

---

[159] 14 C.F.R. § 1.1.
[160] Drone Prize 2014, http://www.droneprize.com/

considered exempt from commercial operation regulations? If UAS are considered "aircraft" and therefore subject to 14 C.F.R. Part 91, then should not 14 C.F.R. § 119.1 apply to UAS as well? Section 119.1 says that Part 119 "applies to each person operating or intending to operate civil aircraft, [a]s an air carrier or commercial operator, or both, in air commerce,"[161] and then § 119.1 goes on to say that "[c]rop dusting, seeding, spraying, and bird chasing[,]" [162] or "[a]erial photography or survey"[163] are exempt from the commercial operator regulations.[164] Is UA aerial photography just a "commercial operation" not under commercial operator regulations?

The 2007 Notice creates the interesting hypothetical situation where a commercial pilot, operating a manned aircraft that is certified under a SAC-EC that allows aerial work,[165] is permitted as a *manned*

---

[161] 14 C.F.R. § 119.1(a).
[162] *Id.* § 119.1(e)(4)(i).
[163] *Id.* § 119.1(e)(4)(iii).
[164] *Id.* § 119.1(e).
[165] *See* FAA Legal Interpretation to Gregory Winton from Mark W. Bury, Acting Assistant Chief Counsel (Feb. 14, 2013), *available at* http://www.faa.gov/about/office_org/headquarters_offices/agc/pol_adjudication/agc 200/Interpretations/data/interps/2013/Winton-AviationLawFirm%20-%20(2013)%20Legal%20Interpretation.pdf ("[T]his operation would only be in compliance with § 91.319(a) if your client is (1) operating the aircraft with an experimental certificate for the purpose for which the certificate was issued, and (2) carrying only the operator's . . . property while conducting the aerial work operations.").

aircraft to go out and do aerial photography under 14 C.F.R. § 119 and 14 C.F.R. § 21, but if he were to land and start flying a UA for commercial aerial photography, he could not because of the 2007 policy statement, not because of the regulations.

c. THE 2008 POLICY STATEMENT FOR COA OR SAC-EC APPLICATIONS.

In March 2008, the FAA created another policy statement ("2008 Policy") called Interim Operational Approval Guidance 08-01[166] as guidance on analyzing applications for COAs for public aircraft or SAC-EC for civil aircraft.[167] The 2005 policy had seven definitions, while this statement added six additional new definitions while expanding the definition of pilot in command ("PIC")[168] to include the PIC holding " the appropriate category, class, and type rating, if appropriate[.]"[169] The 2008 Policy echoed an almost identical definition for Unmanned Aircraft as the 2005 Policy that everything

---

[166] FED. AVIATION ADMIN., AIR-160 Interim Operational Approval Guidance 08-01, Unmanned Aircraft Systems Operations in the U. S. National Airspace System 1 (2008) [hereinafter "2008 Policy Statement"], http://www.faa.gov/about/office_org/headquarters_offices/ato/service_units/systemops/aaim/organizations/uas/coa/faq/media/uas_guidance08-01.pdf

[167] See id. at 2.

[168] See id. at 3.

[169] Id.

that is basically considered an aircraft under 14 C.F.R. § 1.1, except a balloon, is covered.[170] What is strikingly *not* in the definitions is "business purposes" from the 2007 Notice. This 2008 Policy is much more robust than the 2005 Policy and there are many additions.

Most notable, is the guidance's requirement of the pilot having an FAA pilot's certificate if the FAA *determines* that the "location of the planned operations, mission profile, size of the [UA]," require it or if the UA will be flown out of sight.[171] A pilot's certificate is always required if the pilot is to fly the UA in "[a]ll operations approved for conduct in Class A, C, D, and E airspace. All operations conducted under IFR (FAA instrument rating required). All operations approved for nighttime operations. All operations conducted at joint use or public airfields. All operations conducted beyond line of sight."[172]

The 2008 Policy then states that the FAA may require the UA pilot to have specific airplane category and class ratings in manned aircraft, depending on the type of UA to be certified.[173]

---

[170] *See id.* at 3.
[171] *Id.* at 14.
[172] *Id.* at 15.
[173] *See id.*

Another thing to point out is that the PIC may operate *without* a pilot's certificate as long as the PIC has passed an FAA Private Pilot knowledge test and the PIC flies only in Class G, within visual line of sight of 1 nautical mile, within 400 feet above the ground, in a sparsely populated location, from a privately owned airfield or military installation or off-airport location, during daylight, and not within 5 nautical miles of an airport or heliport.[174]

It is controversial how the policy requires that a UA must have a PIC and also an observer which both shall maintain a 2nd class medical. The FAA's reasons for the 2nd class medical are that (1) no commercial pilot has anything less than a 2nd class and (2) 2nd class vision requirements will be needed as opposed to 3rd class because some UA pilots will have to maintain visual contact with the UA.[175]

The counter arguments to the FAA's position would be that even though all commercial pilots are required to have 2nd class medicals, analogously, a flight instructor professional being paid money to train

---

[174] *See id.*

[175] *See* FED. AVIATION ADMIN, Unmanned Aircraft Pilot Medical Certification Requirements 7, *available at* http://www.fas.org/irp/program/collect/ua-pilot.pdf

a student only requires a 3rd class medical.[176] Furthermore, the 2nd class requirement does not further the FAA's mission of promoting safety because a UA pilot with better vision[177] on the ground flying a small UA within LOS has (1) better surrounding vision than the view from a cockpit and (2) cannot do as much damage as a private pilot with a 3rd class medical[178] flying a 6,800 pound twin engine[179] Cessna 401 or a student pilot that could be only sixteen years old[180] on his or her first solo[181] flight.

However, as of January 23, 2015, the FAA is allowing pilots to operate UAS under 333 exemptions, talked about later, with only a third class medical. This area is constantly evolving.

---

[176] *See* 14 C.F.R. § 61.23(a)(3)(iv).
[177] *See* 14 C.F.R. § 67.203 (a second class medical requires, "[d]istant visual acuity of 20/20[.]").
[178] *See* 14 C.F.R. § 67.303 (a third class medical requires, "[d]istant visual acuity of 20/40[.]").
[179] *See* 14 C.F.R. § 61.23(a)(3)(i).
[180] *See* 14 C.F.R. § 61.83(a).
[181] *See* 14 C.F.R. § 61.23(a)(3)(iii).

d. THE 2013 POLICY STATEMENT ON AIRWOTHINESS CERTIFICATION OF UNMANNED AIRCRAFT

The FAA created in 2008 a policy statement called Airworthiness Certification of Unmanned Aircraft Systems.[182] This policy statement was updated in 2011[183] and later in 2013.[184] Currently, the statement calls for the aircraft operator to obtain an airworthiness certificate[185] or special flight permit ("SFP").[186] Civil aircraft operators can obtain an SAC-EC for the purposes of research and development, market survey, or crew training.[187] The UA must be registered,[188] and the unique registration number for the aircraft and nationality must be on the aircraft.[189] The applicant is to develop a maintenance and

---

[182] *See* FED. AVIATION ADMIN., ORDER 8130.34, Airworthiness Certification of Unmanned Aircraft Systems (2008),
http://www.faa.gov/about/office_org/headquarters_offices/ato/service_units/systemops/aaim/organizations/uas/coa/faq/media/Order_8130.34.pdf

[183] *See* FED. AVIATION ADMIN., ORDER 8130.34B, Airworthiness Certification of Unmanned Aircraft Systems and Optionally Piloted Aircraft (2011),
http://www.faa.gov/documentLibrary/media/Order/8130.34B.pdf

[184] *See* FED. AVIATION ADMIN., ORDER 8130.34C, Airworthiness Certification of Unmanned Aircraft Systems and Optionally Piloted Aircraft (2013) [hereinafter "2013 SAC-EC Policy"],
http://www.faa.gov/documentLibrary/media/Order/8130.34C.pdf

[185] *See id.* at 2-4; *see also id.* at 3-1.

[186] *See id.* at 2-4; *see also* 14 C.F.R. § 21.199.

[187] *See id.* at 2-4; *see also id.* 3-7.

[188] *See id.* at 2-1.

[189] Oddly, the size was left out even though it was listed in the section title. Compare with *supra* Order 8130.34B on page 2-3 for what the FAA mistakenly left out; 14 C.F.R. § 45.29.

inspection program for the aircraft,[190] a safety checklist,[191] operations manual, a training curriculum,[192] and the applicant is to show a pilot's certificate and a medical certificate.[193] The frequency spectrum that the UAS will operate on must be approved by the Federal Communications Commission.[194]

Once the application is sent in, the "FAA team typically consists of ASIs and specialists from AIR-200, AFS-80, the Aircraft Maintenance Division (AFS-300), the geographically responsible FSDO," and others will conduct a review of the documents and then conduct an on-site inspection which will hopefully result in an issuance of a SAC-EC or SFP.[195] A flight test will immediately happen after the issuance.[196] Interestingly, the FAA allows for the creation of designated manufacturing representatives to issue special flight permits solely for flight testing.[197]

---

[190] *See* 2013 SAC-EC Policy, *supra* note184, at 3-3.

[191] *See id.* at 3-3.

[192] *See id.* 3-4.

[193] *See id.*

[194] *See id.*

[195] *See id.* at 3-3 to 3-4.

[196] *See id.* at 3-4.

[197] *See id.* at 2-3; *see also* FED. AVIATION ADMIN., Order 8000.372A, Unmanned Aircraft Systems (UAS) Designated Airworthiness Representatives (DAR) for UAS Certification at UAS Test,

The SAC-EC has operating limitations and they are governed by 14 C.F.R. § 91.319.[198] No SAC-EC aircraft can operate outside the purpose of the certificate's issuance (crew training, etc.), carry property or person for compensation or hire, over densely populated areas or in congested airways, at night or under instrument flight rules (unless authorized to operate night or IFR), and any other limitations that the FAA deems necessary.[199] Also, before the UA is flown for people, (market surveys, sales demonstrations, or customer crew training), it must have logged at least 50 hours of training, and/or research & development under a SAC-EC or COA, unless FAA authorizes a reduction.[200] A SAC-EC is good for a year[201] and a SFP for as long as it is specified.[202]

e. THE 2013 POLICY STATEMENT ON UNMANNED OPERATION APPROVALS

On January 22, 2013, the FAA issued Order 8900.207 with the subject of Unmanned Aircraft Systems ("UAS") Operational

---

http://www.faa.gov/regulations_policies/orders_notices/index.cfm/go/document.information/documentID/1026428

[198] *See id.* at 3-7.

[199] *See* 14 C.F.R. § 91.319 (a)-(i).

[200] *See id.* at 3-6.

[201] *See id.* at 3-7.

[202] *Id.*

58

Approval,[203] but this policy statement was superseded by Order 8900.227 on July 30, 2013.[204] This policy statement is really a summation of all the other policy statements; however, there are a few new things. This statement calls for the FAA's legal counsel to determine if an entity applying for a COA is public or not.[205] "All accidents and incidents involving fatalities, injuries, property damage, and fly-away by civil aircraft and those public aircraft" are to be reported.[206] There is a provision for the issuance of emergency COAs,[207] the clarification that even if the UA is *civil* and has a SAC, that it still must obtain a COA for commercial or civil activities.[208] Some UA *may* have to have a flight termination system (could a parachute work?) to protect the public.[209] UA, if authorized under the COA, can fly in Class A, C, D, E airspace.[210] Oddly, UA must have specific approval to spray or drop objects even though the

---

[203] *See* FED. AVIATION ADMIN., Notice 8900.207, UNMANNED AIRCRAFT SYSTEMS (UAS) OPERATIONAL APPROVAL (2013), http://www.faa.gov/documentlibrary/media/notice/n%208900.207.pdf
[204] *See* FED. AVIATION ADMIN., NOTICE 8900.227, UNMANNED AIRCRAFT SYSTEMS (UAS) OPERATIONAL APPROVAL (2013) [hereinafter "2013 Policy Statement"], http://www.faa.gov/documentLibrary/media/Notice/N_8900.227.pdf
[205] *See id.* at 4.
[206] *Id.* at 5.
[207] *See id.* at 6.
[208] *See id.* at 4.
[209] *See id.* at 12.
[210] *See id.* at 13.

regulations[211] don't require that of manned aircraft.[212] UA can be permitted to fly at night,[213] over densely populated areas, heavily trafficked roads, or open air assemblies of people, provided the UA has adequate risk mitigation.[214]

Pilots are to have a private pilot certificate or FAA recognized equivalent when operating anywhere above 400 feet, in Class A, C, D, E airspace, at night, or when the FAA feels it is needed.[215] A UA can be piloted without a private pilot's certificate if the pilot has completed private pilot ground school and has taken the written exam, flies the UA during the day, in a sparsely populated area, in class G airspace below 400 feet and within 1/2 mile laterally, within visual line of sight of the pilot, and not within 5 nautical miles of an airport.[216] The pilot, observer, and supplemental pilots must have a second class medical.[217] The pilot must maintain currency in the

---

[211] 14 C.F.R. § 91.15 ("No pilot in command of a civil aircraft may allow any object to be dropped from that aircraft in flight that creates a hazard to persons or property. However, this section does not prohibit the dropping of any object if reasonable precautions are taken to avoid injury or damage to persons or property.").
[212] *See id.* at 14.
[213] *See id.* at 15.
[214] *See id.* at 14.
[215] *See id.* at 19-20.
[216] *See id.* at 21.
[217] *See id.* at 21-22.

specific UA by doing three take off and landings within the previous 90 days.[218] For operations requiring a certificated pilot, the pilot must have undertaken a biannual flight review and also maintain currency in a *manned* aircraft, three take off and landings for the day or all three to a stop for night currency.[219]

f. THE 2014 POLICY STATEMENT ON THE INTERPRETATION OF THE SPECIAL RULE FOR MODEL AIRCRAFT

On June 25, 2014, the FAA posted in the Federal Register an "Interpretation of the Special Rule for Model Aircraft[.]"[220] This interpretation created such a flurry of comments (33,585)[221] that the FAA extended the comment period.[222] The interpretation stated that AC 91-57 was clarified by the 2007 Policy Statement[223] and then explained Section 336 of the FAA Modernization and Reform Act of

---

[218] *See id.* at 21.
[219] *See id.*
[220] *See* Interpretation of the Special Rule for Model Aircraft, 79 Fed. Reg. 36,171 (proposed June 25, 2014), [hereinafter "2014 Model Aircraft Policy Statement"], *available at* http://www.gpo.gov/fdsys/pkg/FR-2014-06-25/pdf/2014-14948.pdf
[221] Interpretation of the Special Rule for Model Aircraft, *available at* http://www.regulations.gov/#!docketDetail;D=FAA-2014-0396
[222] Notice of interpretation with request for comment; Extension of comment period, 79 Fed. Reg. 43,240 (published July 25, 2014), *available at* http://www.regulations.gov/#!documentDetail;D=FAA-2014-0396-0781
[223] *See* 2007 Notice, *supra* note 149.

2012[224] defines model aircraft as an unmanned aircraft "(1) capable of sustained flight in the atmosphere; (2) flown within visual line of sight of the person operating the aircraft; and (3) flown for hobby or recreational purposes" which are "exempt from future FAA rulemaking action specifically[.]"[225] The FAA went on to state that for a model aircraft to avoid future rulemaking, it could not be flown using goggles designed for First Person View (FPV).[226] The FAA goes on to indirectly carve out a new class of non-model/ non-commercial aircraft by saying,

> [F]lights that are in furtherance of a business, or incidental to a person's business, would not be a hobby or recreation flight. . . . Although they are not commercial operations conducted for compensation or hire, such operations do not qualify as a hobby or recreation flight because of the nexus between the operator's business and the operation of the aircraft.[227]

Why did the FAA have to publish this interpretation? One of the reasons was that pilots were coming up with all sorts of creative ways to make money off flying the drone. They would not make money for

---

[224] *See* FMRA, *infra* note 233.

[225] *See* Interpretation of the Special Rule for Model Aircraft, 79 Fed. Reg. 36,171; 36,173 (proposed June 25, 2014), *available at* http://www.gpo.gov/fdsys/pkg/FR-2014-06-25/pdf/2014-14948.pdf

[226] *Id.* at 36,173.

[227] *Id.*

the flight directly but on the things related to the flight. For example, a realtor would take a shot of the house for free so that it would be more marketable; thus, making more money off the sale of the house. Another example is where a photographer could charge an extremely high rate for "editing" the photos or videos from the free flight to sell to individuals. This table is taken from the interpretation.[228]

Hobby or recreation	Not hobby or recreation
-Flying a model aircraft at the local model aircraft club. -Taking photographs with a model aircraft for personal use. -Using a model aircraft to move a box from point to point without any kind of compensation. -Viewing a field to determine whether crops need water when they are grown for personal enjoyment.	-Receiving money for demonstrating aerobatics with a model aircraft. -A realtor using a model aircraft to photograph a property that he is trying to sell and using the photos in the property's real estate listing. -A person photographing a property or event and selling the photos to someone else. -Delivering packages to people for a fee. -Determining whether crops need to be watered that are grown as part of commercial farming operation.

---

[228] *Id.* at 36,174.

In the regulations, the test to determine if a pilot is operating as a commercial operator is "whether the carriage by air is merely incidental to the person's other business or is, in itself, a major enterprise for profit."[229] What is interesting here is that this policy statement prohibits incidental business for unmanned aircraft while the regulations say, "[a] private pilot may, for compensation or hire, act as pilot in command of an aircraft in connection with any business or employment if: (1) The flight is only incidental to that business or employment; and (2) The aircraft does not carry passengers or property for compensation or hire."[230]

The FAA then went on to say, "The FAA could apply several regulations in part 91 when determining whether to take enforcement action against a model aircraft operator for endangering the NAS."[231] The FAA listed sections 91.13, 91.15, 91.113, 91.126, 91.135, 91.126, 91.127, 91.129(a), 91.135, 91.137, 91.145 as regulations that would most likely be violated, however, "other parts of the regulations, may

---

[229] 14 C.F.R. § 1.1.
[230] 14 C.F.R. § 61.113(b); Letter from Mark Bury to Randy Hurst (May 17, 2913), http://www.faa.gov/about/office_org/headquarters_offices/agc/pol_adjudication/agc200/interpretations/data/interps/2013/randy%20hurst%20-%20(2013)%20legal%20interpretation.pdf
[231] *Id.* at 36,176.

64

apply to model aircraft operations, depending on the particular

circumstances of the operation. The regulations cited above are not

intended to be an exhaustive list of rules that could apply to model

aircraft operations."[232]

---

[232] *Id.*

Chapter Four: The FAA Modernization and Reform Act of 2012

President Obama signed the FAA Modernization and Reform Act of 2012 ("FMRA") on February 14, 2012,[233] which mandates the FAA to do a "phased-in approach"[234] to the integration of civil unmanned aircraft[235] into the national airspace system based upon a comprehensive plan.[236] This law is forward looking and mandates the FAA to create regulations for unmanned aircraft but not to create regulations for model aircraft.

---

[233] FAA Modernization and Reform Act of 2012, Pub. L. No. 112-95, 126 Stat. 11 (2012) [hereinafter "FMRA"]. *available at* http://www.gpo.gov/fdsys/pkg/PLAW-112publ95/pdf/PLAW-112publ95.pdf

[234] *Id.* § 332(a)(2)(C), 126 Stat. at 73.

[235] *See id.* § 331(8), 126 Stat. at 72, ("'[U]nmanned aircraft' means an aircraft that is operated without the possibility of direct human intervention from within or on the aircraft.").

[236] *See id.* §§ 331-336, 126 Stat. at 72-78. (This was fulfilled by the 2013 Roadmap mentioned earlier).

The FMRA mandates the creation of regulations dealing with the operation and certification[237] of unmanned aircraft. It also mandates for standards, requirements, licensing, and registration for unmanned aircraft pilots.[238] Interestingly, Congress mandates the FAA to create the unmanned aircraft regulations by a notice in the Federal Register and the publishing of the final rule.[239] Also, Congress wants an update to the 2007 Policy that the FAA issued that has prevented the commercial UA industry.[240] Does this mean that Congress believes that the FAA does *not* have any regulations pertaining to UA?

To help develop standards and understand what needs to be done for integration, the FAA is to create six test sites to test the UA.[241] In addition to these six test sites, the FAA is to create areas in the Alaskan Arctic[242] "where small unmanned aircraft may operate 24

---

[237] *See id.* § 332(a)(2)(A)(i), 126 Stat. at 73.
[238] *See id.* § 332(a)(2)(A)(iii), 126 Stat. at 73.
[239] *See id.* § 332(b); 126 Stat. at 74.
[240] *See id.* § 332(b)(1)-(3), 126 Stat. at 74.
[241] *See id.* § 332(c), 126 Stat. at 74.
[242] *See id.* § 331(1), 126 Stat. at 72, ("The term ''Arctic'' means the United States zone of the Chukchi Sea, Beaufort Sea, and Bering Sea north of the Aleutian chain.").

hours per day for research and commercial[243] purposes."[244] The deadline for all of this to be completed is September 30, 2015.[245]

For public[246] aircraft, the FMRA calls for guidance[247] to be created within 270 days for the operation of public UA,[248] with a deadline, December 31, 2015, for the creation of regulations on the operation and certification of public UA in the airspace.[249] The FMRA calls for the FAA to expedite the certification of authorization ("COA")[250] process for public entities, that the COA needs to be obtained only once as long as the public aircraft is operated below 4.4 pounds, is operated within line of sight, is below 400 feet, during the day, within

---

[243] Press, *FAA Opens the Arctic to Commercial Small Unmanned Aircraft*, SUAS NEWS (Sept. 27, 2013), http://www.suasnews.com/2013/09/25308/faa-opens-the-arctic-to-commercial-small-unmanned-aircraft/, (On September 13, 2013,"[t]he Westward Wind, [a boat] chartered by energy giant ConocoPhillips, carried four Insitu Scan Eagle UAS to perform marine mammal and ice surveys necessary to meet environmental and safety rules before drilling on the sea floor.").

[244] FMRA, Pub. L. No. 112-95, § 332(d)(1), 126 Stat. at 75.

[245] *See id.* § 332(a)(3), 126 Stat. at 73.

[246] *See id.* § 331(2), 126 Stat. at 72, ("The term 'public unmanned aircraft system' means an unmanned aircraft system that meets the qualifications and conditions required for operation of a public aircraft (as defined in section 40102 of title 49, United States Code).").

[247] In contrast to unmanned civil aircraft which will prospectively have regulations.

[248] *See id.* § 334(a), 126 Stat. at 76.

[249] *See id.* § 334(b), 126 Stat. at 76.

[250] *See id.* § 331(2), 126 Stat. at 72, ("The terms 'certificate of waiver' and 'certificate of authorization' mean a Federal Aviation Administration grant of approval for a specific flight operation.").

class G airspace, and 5 miles away from any airport.[251] It should be noted that since the FMRA went into effect, the FAA has entered into a memorandum of understanding between the Department of Justice, Office of Justice Programs, and National Institute of Justice to help non-federal law enforcement agencies operate UA and which also lays out looser qualifications than the FMRA.[252]

The FMRA specifically prohibits the FAA from creating any rule or regulation for model aircraft.[253] The FMRA defines "model aircraft" but *only* for the purpose of defining the *scope* of the FAA's regulatory authority with respect to model aircraft. The FMRA says that model aircraft are "flown within visual line of sight[,]"[254] are strictly recreational, are below 55 pounds unless otherwise authorized, communicate with the airport operator if the model is to be flown within 5 miles of an airport,[255] and are operated in accordance within a "community-based set of safety guidelines and within the

---

[251] *See id.* § 334(c), 126 Stat. at 76-77.
[252] *See* Memorandum of Understanding Between Federal Aviation Administration, Unmanned Aircraft Systems Integration Office and t U.S. Department of Justice, Office of Justice Programs, National Institute of Justice Concerning Operation of Unmanned Aircraft Systems by Law Enforcement Agencies, http://www.alea.org/assets/pressReleases/assets/1805/DOJ%20FAA%20MOU.pdf
[253] FMRA, Pub. L. No. 112-95, §336(a)(1)-(5), 126 Stat. at 77.
[254] *Id.* § 336(c)(2), 126 Stat. at 78.
[255] *See id.* §336(a)(1)-(5), 126 Stat. at 77.

programming of a nationwide community-based organization[("CBO").]" [256] Currently, the Academy of Model Aeronautics ("AMA") is the only CBO that is working with the FAA and has signed a memorandum of understanding with FAA. [257] The AMA has a National Model Aircraft Safety Code. [258] This presents a problem if model aircraft, within the scope of the FMRA, were being used in such a way as to endanger the national airspace. How could the FAA use any regulations against those model aircraft if the FMRA specifically forbid any type of regulation on those aircraft?

The FMRA attempts to answer that question by saying, "[n]othing in this section shall be construed to limit the authority of the Administrator to pursue enforcement action against persons operating model aircraft who endanger the safety of the national airspace system."[259] How is this exception prevented from swallowing the rule against creating any rules against model aircraft? The FAA could create a regulation from just copying and pasting a part of the FMRA

---

[256] *Id.* § 336(a)(2), 126 Stat. at 77.

[257] *See* Patrick Egan, *MOU between the FAA and AMA*, sUAS News (Jan. 11, 2014), http://www.suasnews.com/2014/01/26919/moa-between-the-faa-and-ama

[258] *See* Academy of Model Aeronautics National Model Aircraft Safety Code, AMA, http://www.modelaircraft.org/files/105.PDF

[259] FMRA, Pub. L. No. 112-95, §336(b), 126 Stat. at 77.

and say that no model aircraft flyer shall "endanger the safety of the national airspace system" but this creates the next problem which illustrates the exception swallowing the rule; what is "endanger?"

Section 333 of the FMRA is what has been causing a lot of buzz lately. This section allows for UAS to be exempted from aircraft regulations. A more detailed discussion is later in the book.

Finally, the Brookings Institute points out, "There is no penalty for tardiness in the statute, for example. If the FAA misses a must-do-by date, the agency may have to reckon with congressional pressure and stakeholder disapproval. But there's no formal compliance mechanism to hurry the agency along."[260]

---

[260] Wells C. Bennett, *Unmanned at Any Speed: Bringing Drones into Our National Airspace*, ISSUES IN GOVERNANCE STUD., Dec. 2012, at 3, *available at* http://www.brookings.edu/~/media/research/files/papers/2012/12/14%20drones%20 bennett/1214_drones_bennett.pdf

CHAPTER FIVE: THE 2013 ROADMAP

The Department of Transportation ("DOT") first released its comprehensive plan to integrate UAS[261] with the FAA releasing their UAS integration roadmap plan[262] about a month later. Only the FAA roadmap will be focused on in this book. The FAA was charged under the FAA Modernization and Reform Act of 2012[263] to create a roadmap on how to integrate unmanned aircraft into the national airspace. This roadmap had been in the making since at least July 2013 because referenced in the roadmap is Notice 8900.207 which was cancelled by Notice 8900.227 in July but was never updated in the roadmap. This roadmap outlines the FAA's future plans and the process by which the FAA plans are to be achieved.

---

[261] DEP'T OF TRANSP., Unmanned Aircraft Systems (Uas) Comprehensive Plan (2013), http://www.faa.gov/about/office_org/headquarters_offices/agi/reports/media/UAS_Comprehensive_Plan.pdf
[262] *See* FED. AVIATION ADMIN., Integration of Civil Unmanned Aircraft Systems (UAS) in the National Airspace System (NAS) Roadmap (2013) [hereinafter "FAA Roadmap"], http://www.faa.gov/about/initiatives/uas/media/uas_roadmap_2013.pdf
[263] FMRA, *Infra* note 233.

The FAA roadmap requires that test site operators establish a privacy policy for operations at UA test sites, make available the privacy policy to the public, and provide a means for comment on that privacy policy. [264] Interestingly, the roadmap says "The term 'Operator' is used here as defined by the FAA for passenger/cargo carrying and other 'for hire and compensation' operations . . . . One outcome of this effort will be to establish which UA operations will or will not require an Operator Certificate." [265] It seems that the new regulations pertaining to small UA ("sUAS") will be in 14 C.F.R. § 107[266] and will allow operators to operate under the regulations and not have to "conduct operations under either a COA or the constraints of an experimental certificate. This will allow operators and the FAA to shift the focus of resources to solutions that will better enable UAS integration."[267]

---

[264] *See id.* at 11-12.
[265] *Id.* at 51.
[266] *See id.* at 58-59.
[267] *Id.* at 34.

CHAPTER SIX: THE UNMANNED AIRCRAFT CERTIFICATION PROCESS

With all the policy statements talked about, it can be a little confusing as to what the FAA believes is needed to fly the UA. The current view of how UA are being integrated is that of having the UA conform to existing manned aircraft regulations until new regulations are created that fully address UA. [268] The whole certification process for civil manned aircraft is outside the scope of this book but a few things must be noted. To fly a *civil*, non-model, unmanned aircraft in the national airspace, the aircraft must have an airworthiness certificate[269] unless it is exempted from this requirement by being granted an exemption under Section 333 of the FMRA. Airworthiness certificates are broken up into: (1) standard

---

[268] *See* FAA Roadmap, *supra* note 262, at 28 ("UAS training standards will mirror manned aircraft training standards to the maximum extent possible[.]").
[269] *See* 49 U.S.C. § 44711(a)(1); 14 C.F.R. § 91.203(a)(1).

74

airworthiness certificates[270]and (2) special airworthiness certificates.[271] The special airworthiness certificate grouping is where civil UAS are being certificated.

The FAA's plan to put UA into the skies is to accommodate, integrate, and evolve.[272] A UA is viewed as part of the Unmanned Aerial System ("UAS") and that is actually what has to obtain certification. Currently, there is no UA pilot's certificate; therefore, traditional manned aircraft pilot's certificates are being required.[273] There are only six ways that the UAS can be operated: (1) a public aircraft with a Certificate of Waiver/ Authorization ("COA"), (2) a civil aircraft with a Special Airworthiness Certificate ("SAC") for the UAS and a COA for operations, (3) a civil aircraft with a 333 exemption and a COA, (4) be sponsored to fly in restricted, prohibited, or warning airspace with the permission of the controlling agency,[274]

---

[270] *See* 14 C.F.R. § 21.21.
[271] *See* 14 C.F.R. §§ 21.25; 21.185; 21.191; 21.193; 21.195; 21.197.
[272] *See id.* at 21.
[273] UA flight experience cannot be used towards obtaining a manned aircraft pilot's license *See* FED. AVIATION ADMIN., N 8900.258, Logging of Unmanned Aircraft Systems Pilot Time (2014), http://www.faa.gov/documentlibrary/media/notice/n_8900.258.pdf
[274] 2008 Policy Statement, *supra* note 166, at 4 ("In general, specific authorization to conduct unmanned aircraft operations in the NAS outside of active Restricted, Prohibited, or Warning Area airspace must be requested by the applicant. Airspace

(5) flying in oceanic warning areas or FAA controlled international airspace, [275] or (6) fly as a model aircraft. Flying in restricted, prohibited, [276] warning, oceanic, or FAA controlled international airspace is beyond the scope of this book and will not be discussed.

The FAA has approved about 1,346 COAs from 2007 to October, 2012 with 50% of them for the Department of Defense. [277] "Applications for a COA are accepted from entities that intend to conduct public aircraft, civil, or commercial operations."[278] The reason public and civil aircraft need COA's is that unmanned aircraft are not in compliance with the FAR's, for example § 91.113 requires "see and avoid;" and UA need alternative means to comply. Therefore, public, civil, or commercial aircraft must apply for "a certificate of waiver authorizing the operation of [the] aircraft in deviation from any rule

inside buildings or structures is not considered to be part of the NAS and is not regulated.").
[275] See 2013 Policy Statement, *supra* note 204, at 3-4.
[276] See FED. AVIATION ADMIN., Order JO 7400.8V, Special Use Airspace (2013), http://www.faa.gov/documentlibrary/media/order/sua.pdf
[277] Bruce LaCour & Mike Wilson, *NextGen – An UpdateTalk*, FED. AVIATION ADMIN., 72 (June 13, 2013), http://www.faa.gov/about/office_org/field_offices/fsdo/orl/local_more/media/fy13summit/nextgen_mco_safety_summit.pdf
[278] See 2013 Policy Statement, *supra* note 204, at 4.

listed in . . . [§ 91.905].[279] if the Administrator finds that the proposed operation can be safely conducted under the terms of that certificate of waiver."[280]

A. PUBLIC AIRCRAFT APPLY FOR A CERTIFICATE OF AUTHORIZATION OR WAIVER

Airworthiness certificate requirements apply only to civil aircraft;[281] therefore, public aircraft use their own standards[282] for pilot certification, medical certification, and airworthiness of their UA. The public entity applies to the FAA to only *operate* its aircraft under a COA.[283] Conversely, civil aircraft cannot create their own standards but must follow the ones prescribed[284] by the FAA. If the public entity applying does not have any of its own standards, the FAA recommends *voluntarily* complying with the standards in Order 8900.227 and the regulations for civil aircraft.[285] Public aircraft must

---

[279] Many of the regulations in part 91 can be waived including the "see and avoid" requirement.
[280] 14 C.F.R. § 91.903(a).
[281] *See supra* note 269.
[282] *Id.* at 5.
[283] *See id.* at 4.
[284] *See* 2013 SAC-EC Policy, *supra* note 184, at 1-2.
[285] *See* 2013 Policy Statement, *supra* note204, at 4.

be carrying out a government function. "'[G]overnmental function' means an activity undertaken by a government, such as national defense, intelligence missions, firefighting, search and rescue, law enforcement (including transport of prisoners, detainees, and illegal aliens), aeronautical research, or biological or geological resource management."[286] The FAA has determined that education is not a government function for purposes of 49 U.S.C. §40125(a)(2). Therefore, a public university cannot obtain a COA to operate a flight school;[287] however, it could obtain a COA to conduct other types of government functions such as atmosphere research.[288] The government function is determined by the FAA on a case by case basis.

Any group of *civilian* volunteers performing the same function as a government function, *i.e.* search and rescue, might be asked to obtain a

---

[286] 49 U.S.C. § 40125(a)(2).

[287] Memo from Jim Williams to Mark Bury, 3, (July 3, 2014), https://www.faa.gov/about/office_org/headquarters_offices/agc/pol_adjudication/agc 200/Interpretations/data/interps/2014/Williams-AFS-80%20education%20-%20(2014)%20Legal%20Interpretation.pdf

[288] *See* Memo from Jim Williams to Mark Bury on the Clarification of June 13, 2014 Interpretation on Research Using UAS, 1 (July 3, 2014), https://www.faa.gov/about/office_org/headquarters_offices/agc/pol_adjudication/agc 200/Interpretations/data/interps/2014/Williams-AFS-80%20Clarification%20-%20(2014)%20Legal%20Interpretation.pdf

COA as evidenced by email from an aviation safety inspector to Texas Equusearch saying their search and rescue operation was "an illegal operation regardless if it [was] below 400ft AGL, VLOS or doing volunteer SAR."[289] Texas Equusearch tried to resolve the situation with a letter to the FAA[290] but was forced to petition the D.C Circuit Court of Appeals to review the email[291] The D.C. Court of Appeals dismissed the case because the email:

> [D]id not represent the consummation of the agency's decision making process, nor did it give rise to any legal consequences. . . . The email at issue is not a formal cease-and-desist letter representing the agency's final conclusion, after following the procedures set out in 14 C.F.R. pt. 13, that an entity has violated the law, which we have previously found sufficient to constitute final agency action. . . . Rather, given the absence of any identified legal consequences flowing from the challenged email, this case falls within the usual rule that this court lacks authority to review a claim "where 'an agency merely expresses its view of what the law requires of a party, even if that view is adverse to the party.[292]

---

[289] Petition for Review at 8, *Tex. Equusearch Mounted Search and Recovery Team v. Fed. Aviation. Admin*, No. 14-1061 (D.C. Cir. Apr. 21, 2014), *available at* http://www.kramerlevin.com/files/upload/tes-v-faa.pdf

[290] *See* Letter from Texas EquuSearch to the Chief Counsel of the FAA (March 17, 2014), http://www.kramerlevin.com/files/upload/TES-Letter.pdf

[291] *See* Petition for Review, *supra* note 289, at 8.

[292] *Tex. Equusearch Mounted Search and Recovery Team v. Fed. Aviation. Admin*, No. 14-1061, slip op. at 1-2 (D.C. Cir July 18, 2014) (citations omitted) (quoting another source), *available at* https://nppa.org/sites/default/files/Equusearch%20v%20FAA%20Order%2007-18-14.pdf

Any civilian group performing any type of function that has been traditionally a government function should check with a competent aviation attorney before conducting activities.

The FAA and the Department of Justice's National Institute of Justice have established an agreement that lets "law enforcement organizations [] receive a COA for training and performance evaluation. When the organization has shown proficiency in flying its UAS, it will receive an operational COA."[293] The agreement allows UA to weigh up to 25 pounds.[294] The COA process is administered by the Air Traffic Organization in the UAS Integration Office using some more policy material[295] to evaluate the COA's. [296]

On February 12, 2014, the FAA updated AC 00-1.1A which deals with public aircraft operations and it said:

> What Constitutes a 'Commercial Purpose' that Removes Someone from [Public Aircraft Operation] Status? In general, the FAA interprets the commercial purpose prohibition in 49 U.S.C. § 40125(a)(1) to mean that there can be no type of

---

[293] *FAA Makes Progress with UAS Integration*, FED. AVIATION ADMIN., http://www.faa.gov/news/updates/?newsId=68004
[294] *See id.*
[295] FED. AVIATION ADMIN., N JO 7210.846, Unmanned Aircraft Operations in the National Airspace System (NAS) (2013), http://www.faa.gov/documentLibrary/media/Notice/N_JO_7210.846.pdf
[296] *See* 2013 Policy Statement, *supra* note 204, at 2, 6.

reimbursement to government entities for [Public Aircraft Operation], except under the one set of specific circumstances described in that section. . . . The statutory prohibition on commercial purpose prevents a government entity from getting paid or reimbursed to operate a [Public Aircraft Operation], not for paying for contracted services.[297]

AC 00-1.1A changed the definition in §40125(a)(1), "the transportation of persons or property for compensation or hire[,]" to "no type of reimbursement[.]" This AC prevents a government agency from operating a UA for profit.

B. CIVIL AIRCRAFT OBTAIN A SPECIAL AIRWORTHINESS CERTIFICATE FOR THE AIRCRAFT AND OPERATE THAT UAS UNDER A CERTIFICATE OF WAIVER OR AUTHORIZATION.

Civil aircraft cannot "self-standardize" like the public aircraft; therefore, all civil aircraft are required to obtain a SAC. These are available *only* to civil airplanes. The civil *aircraft* UAS receives a SAC using Order 8130.34C and then for it to *operate* in the national

---

[297]*See* FED. AVIATION ADMIN., Advisory Circular 00-1.1A, Public Aircraft Operations 8 (2014), *available at* http://www.faa.gov/documentLibrary/media/Advisory_Circular/AC_00-1_1A.pdf

airspace, it must also obtain a COA.[298] The reason I say SAC is that no UAS has to date obtained a standard airworthiness certificate.

The most discussed about SAC is the experimental category ("SAC-EC"). The FAA issued SAC-EC's are only for research and development, market survey and crew training objectives. As of August 2012, 113 have been issued.[299] Pilots will have to hold private pilot certificates depending on the area flown or to have at least completed private pilot ground school. The observer will have to have a private pilot's certificate or to have completed observer training. Both the pilot and observer will need a second-class medical certificate. The SAC-EC has operating limitations and they are governed by 14 C.F.R. § 91.319. Avoiding redundancy, the 2013 Policy Statement previously discussed in the book further explores this area in conjunction with a COA.

---

[298] *See* 2013 Policy Statement, *supra* note 204, at 7; *see also id.* at A-1("COAs are also issued by the ATO as an authorization for civil and commercial operations, provided the aircraft has been issued an airworthiness certificate from the Aircraft Certification Service (AIR).").

[299] *See* FAA Roadmap, *supra* note 262, at 22.

Another category of the special airworthiness certificate is the restricted category [300] ("SAC-RC"). Currently, there are only two aircraft, the AeroVironment Puma and the Insitu ScanEagle, that have this certification, with both having the limitation of "[o]nly for operation in the designated Arctic area as defined by the FAA Modernization and Reform Act of 2012." [301] A restricted category aircraft *can* be used for commercial operations involving agricultural spraying, dusting, seeding, forest and wildlife conservation, aerial surveying, patrolling, or other areas. [302] The Puma and ScanEagle are both type-certificated to do aerial surveillance. [303] The operating limitations for SAC-RC are located in 14 C.F.R. § 91.313 which states that SAC-RC aircraft should not be operated for other than its special purpose; not carrying persons or property for compensation or hire, except for crop dusting, seeding, spraying, and banner towing; not operate over a densely populated area; in a congested airway and near

---

[300] *See* 14 C.F.R. § 21.25; *see also* 2013 Policy Statement, *supra* note 204, at 7.
[301] Graham Warwick, *FAA Type Certifies First UAS for Commercial Ops*, AVIATION WEEK, http://www.aviationweek.com/Article.aspx?id=/article-xml/asd_07_26_2013_p01-01-601023.xml&p=2
[302] 14 C.F.R. § 21.25(b)(1)-(7).
[303] *See One Giant Leap for Unmanned-kind*, FED. AVIATION ADMIN. (July 26, 2013), http://www.faa.gov/news/updates/?newsId=73118&omniRss=news_updatesAoc&cid=101_N_U

a busy airport where air transport is being done, unless the SAC-RC limitations allow for that.[304]

Model aircraft flying is strictly recreational. The model aircraft/ civil aircraft line keeps moving around. One should refer to AC-91-57, the AMA Safety Code,[305] and the 2014 Model Aircraft Interpretation for more information about this evolving area. I left the following text in this book (it is strikethroughed because the FAA changed it position) to be a great educational lesson about dealing with regulatory agencies because I wrote the text back in early 2014. Les Dorr from the FAA further clarified this area in a recent statement:

Farmers may operate an unmanned aircraft over their own property for personal use and should operate safely so as to minimize risk to other aircraft or people or property on the ground. Guidelines for the operation of model aircraft, such as those published by the Academy of Model Aeronautics, may be used by farmers as reference for safe model UAS operations. We expect to publish a proposed rule on small UAS next year that will offer regulations for a wide variety small UAS uses.[306]

---

[304] 14 C.F.R. § 91.313(a)-(g).
[305] *See* Academy of Model Aeronautics National Model Aircraft Safety Code, *infra* note 264, http://www.modelaircraft.org/files/105.PDF
[306] Justin Dougherty, *Oklahoma Farmers Use Drones To Monitor Crops, Cattle*, NEWS9.COM (Nov. 25, 2013), http://www.news9.com/story/24067669/oklahoma-farmers-use-drones-to-monitor-crops-cattle

What does "personal use" mean? Where is the fine line between personal use and commercial use? Can a farmer use the UA to gather data to increase his crop yields? Furthermore, this is Mr. Dorr's statement and not a FAA policy statement or a regulation. Therefore, farmers contemplating doing anything in this murky area should be cautious and seek legal advice.

Moreover, Jim Williams, head of the FAA UAS integration office, said when asked about this statement, "If I'm a modeler and I happen to be a farmer and I operate my model aircraft over my farm, as long as it is done safely, it's none of the business of the FAA what you're doing with the data you collect. We're not getting into that business. Our business is safety, not governing commerce. However, if you formally want an answer from the FAA lawyers, ... it crosses the line from hobby to business." [307]

The FAA published in July 2014 an interpretation on the model aircraft rule that says a farmer's use of a drone for a commercial farming operation prohibits the aircraft from being classified as a

---

[307] sUASNEWS, *2014 sUSB Expo Jim Williams*, YouTube (May 13, 2014), https://www.youtube.com/watch?v=98LF5azVxLg&list=PLS2ntMaPm2ZUhXY2U 87OcvUxRVxnu_y6O

model aircraft.[308] The FAA is continually reclassifying things and changing their position. Anyone who is interested in getting into this area commercially should seek the advice of a competent aviation attorney.

C. SECTION 333 EXEMPTIONS

So how are unmanned aircraft operating commercially if only two UAS have restricted category certificates? The answer comes from Section 333[309] located inside the FMRA. Section 333 reads:

SEC. 333. SPECIAL RULES FOR CERTAIN UNMANNED AIRCRAFT SYSTEMS.

(a) IN GENERAL.—Notwithstanding any other requirement of this subtitle, and not later than 180 days after the date of enactment of this Act, the Secretary of Transportation shall determine if certain unmanned aircraft systems may operate safely in the national airspace system before completion of the plan and rulemaking required by section 332 of this Act or the guidance required by section 334 of this Act

(b) ASSESSMENT OF UNMANNED AIRCRAFT SYSTEMS.—In making the determination under subsection (a), the Secretary shall determine, at a minimum—

(1) which types of unmanned aircraft systems, if any, as a result of their size, weight, speed, operational capability, proximity to airports and populated areas, and operation within visual line of sight do not create a hazard to users of

---

[308] *See* 2014 Model Aircraft Policy Statement, *supra* note 220.
[309] § 333, 126 Stat. 75-76, *available at* http://www.gpo.gov/fdsys/pkg/PLAW-112publ95/pdf/PLAW-112publ95.pdf

the national airspace system or the public or pose a threat to national security; and

(2) whether a certificate of waiver, certificate of authorization, or airworthiness certification under section 44704 of title 49, United States Code, is required for the operation of unmanned aircraft systems identified under paragraph (1).

(c) REQUIREMENTS FOR SAFE OPERATION.—If the Secretary determines under this section that certain unmanned aircraft systems may operate safely in the national airspace system, the Secretary shall establish requirements for the safe operation of such aircraft systems in the national airspace system.

As of February 7, 2015, only 26 exemptions[310] have been granted with a total of 342 petitions already filed.[311] The petitions are granted on a case by case basis. Section 333 allows aircraft to fly under the Federal Aviation Regulations which it can comply with while being exempted from the regulations which are too burdensome to comply with by following the restrictions the FAA imposes and complying with the equivalent standard of safety that their operating manuals provide.

---

[310] *Section 333*, https://www.faa.gov/uas/legislative_programs/section_333/
[311] *FAA Grants Eight More UAS Exemptions*, https://www.faa.gov/news/updates/?newsId=81565

CHAPTER SEVEN: HOW THE FAA ENFORCES ITS REGULATIONS

The FAA has different ways it can enforce the regulations and has a pretty good approach of encouraging safety and compliance.

> It is the role of FAA employees to promote safety through the compliance and enforcement process, as in all agency programs. It is the responsibility of the aviation industry to strive to attain full compliance. Aviation safety depends primarily on voluntary adherence to regulatory requirements. Therefore, compliance is promoted primarily through education, training, and counseling, and only where those efforts have failed, by formal enforcement action.[312]

The FAA published some guidance material directed at state and local law enforcement agencies ("LEA") to support a partnership between them and to help the FAA "pursue enforcement actions to

---

[312] James B. Busey, *Policy on Compliance and Enforcement*, AIRPLANE OWNERS AND PILOT'S ASS'N, http://www.aopa.org/Pilot-Resources/PIC-archive/FAA-Enforcement/FAA-Enforcement.aspx

stop unauthorized or unsafe UAS operations."[313] The document goes on to list how LEA can help the FAA by: (1) witness identification and interviews, (2) identification of operators, (3) viewing and recording the location of the event, (4) identifying sensitive locations, events, or activities, (5) notification, and (6) evidence collection.[314]

For purposes of the scope of this book, only two possible enforcement scenarios will be talked about against a pilot of a UA that is non-military:[315] (1) the pilot is a certificated FAA pilot or the more typical situation of (2) a pilot without a pilot's certificate. The FAA has created regulations[316] on enforcing the regulations in both of these scenarios. Please also keep in mind that the FAA could also come after a company, in addition to the pilot, if the company was flying the drone for compensation or hire.[317]

---

[313] FED. AVIATION ADMIN., Law Enforcement Guidance For Suspected Unauthorized UAS Operations 1 (2015), [hereinafter referred to as "LEA Guidance"], *available at* http://www.faa.gov/uas/regulations_policies/media/FAA_UAS-PO_LEA_Guidance.pdf

[314] *See id.* at 5-7.

[315] Under 49 U.S.C. § 46101(b), the FAA "shall refer a complaint against a member of the armed forces of the United States performing official duties to the Secretary of the department concerned for action."

[316] 14 C.F.R. § 13.11-.23.

[317] 14 C.F.R. § 1.1 ("Commercial operator means a person who, for compensation or hire, engages in the carriage by aircraft in air commerce of persons or property, other

A. ARE UNMANNED AIRCRAFT MODELS OR AIRCRAFT?

This book will be taking the viewpoint of the FAA which necessarily presumes that UA are aircraft as defined in the regulations; therefore, they are subject to the regulations. The FAA's argument is that they have jurisdiction because the definitions of aircraft in 49 U.S.C. § 40102(6), "any contrivance invented, used, or designed to navigate, or fly in, the air[]"[318] and in 14 C.F.R. § 1.1, "a device that is used or intended to be used for flight in the air[,]"[319] are both broad enough so as to encompass UA without explicitly defining them.

Some of the opponents of the FAA and also one National Transportation Safety Board judge believe that:

> [The] FAA historically has not required model aircraft operators to comply with [the] requirements of FAR Part 21, Section 21.1.71 *et seq* and FAR, Part 47, Section 47.3, which require Airworthiness and Registration Certification for an aircraft. The reasonable inference is not that FAA has overlooked the requirements, but[] rather that FAA has

---

than as an air carrier or foreign air carrier or under the authority of Part 375 of this title. Where it is doubtful that an operation is for "compensation or hire", the test applied is whether the carriage by air is merely incidental to the person's other business or is, in itself, a major enterprise for profit.").
[318] 49 U.S.C. § 40102(6).
[319] 14 C.F.R. § 1.1.

distinguished, model aircraft as a class excluded from the regulatory and statutory definitions.

This lower NTSB judge was overruled by the full NTSB board on appeal which held that the definition of aircraft does encompass model aircraft. This ruling will be discussed further in the book.

B. FAA ENFORCEMENT WHERE A CERTIFICATED PILOT IS INVOLVED

In the situations where there is a certificated pilot, the FAA has the options of (1) administratively disposing of the violation with a warning or allow the pilot to voluntarily submit to correction,[320] (2) requiring the certificated pilot to be reexamined for his certificate,[321] (3) suspending or revoking the pilot's certificate,[322] or (4) civil penalties against the pilot.[323] A certificated pilot has spent many hours and dollars obtaining this certificate and the threat of these enforcement mechanisms is to many certificated pilots a deterrent to violating a regulation.

---

[320] *See* 14 C.F.R. §13.11.
[321] *See* 49 U.S.C. § 44709; *see also* 14 C.F.R. §13.19.
[322] *See id.*
[323] *See* 14 C.F.R. §§ 13.14-.16, 29.

The FAA's commercial ban has had the interesting negative safety effect of actually keeping out trained and highly skilled pilots from operating UA because they are more "invested" than non-certificated pilots.

C. FAA ENFORCEMENT WHERE A NON-CERTIFICATED PILOT IS INVOLVED

Typically, the large amount of potential violators do not have any pilot certificate or any interest in becoming a certificated pilot. This forces the FAA to use the civil penalty as its only means of enforcing the regulations. The FAA has a *regulation* that allows the FAA to impose civil penalties for "an individual acting as a pilot[,]"[324] "whether or not that individual holds the respective [pilot's certifcate] issued by the FAA."[325] Douglas Marshall pointed out an interesting situation here for the FAA, "the relevant section of the U.S. Code defines *pilot* as 'an individual who holds a pilot certificate issued under Part 61. . . . [A]n argument could be made that a non-certificate holder would not be subject to even the civil penalty provision of the

---

[324] 14 C.F.R. § 13.18(a)(1); *see also* 49 U.S.C. § 46301(d)(5)(A).
[325] 14 C.F.R. § 13.18(b)(2).

U.S. Code." [326] The *regulations* have a definition that covers non-certificated pilots while the *U.S. Code's* definition covers only certificated pilots. [327] It must be noted that in the recent FAA enforcement against an non-certificated pilot,[328] the attorney for the FAA cited 49 U.S.C. §§ 46301(a)(l), (a)(5), and (d)(2) as grounds for the civil penalty.

D. REGULATIONS THAT THE FAA WILL MOST LIKELY USE FOR ENFORCEMENT OF ITS POLICIES

There are three regulations that will be most likely be used by the FAA in enforcement actions against individuals acting as UA pilots. (1) "No person may operate an aircraft so close to another aircraft as to create a collision hazard[,]" [329] (2) "[w]hen weather conditions permit[,] . . . vigilance shall be maintained by each person operating an aircraft so as to see and avoid other aircraft[,]"[330] and (3) "[n]o person may operate an aircraft in a careless or reckless manner so as to

---

[326] *See* Marshall, *supra* note 125, at 47.
[327] *See* 49 U.S.C. § 46301(d)(1)(C)("'pilot' means an individual who holds a pilot certificate issued under part 61 of title 14, Code of Federal Regulations.").
[328] Order of Assessment, *Administrator v. Pirker*, No. CP-217, (NTSB filed June 27, 2013) http://www.wired.com/images_blogs/threatlevel/2014/10/Complaint.pdf
[329] 14 C.F.R. § 91.111(a).
[330] *Id.* § 91.113(b).

endanger the life or property of another."[331] These are some of the operating rules in part 91 but the FAA has many other "arrows" in its quiver from which to use as enforcement tools. The first one can easily be avoided by not operating near other aircraft, and the second one is also easily avoided by maintaining the UA close by in the line of sight of the pilot. The third standard can be easily violated. This is the basis for the FAA enforcement action against the non-certificated UA pilot Raphael Pirker.

The FAA's 2014 interpretation on the model aircraft rule listed the regulations the FAA felt would most likely be violated by model aircraft flyers.[332] These regulations will be discussed later in the model aircraft section.

---

[331] *Id.* § 91.13(a).
[332] *See* Interpretation of the Special Rule for Model Aircraft, 79 Fed. Reg. 36,171; 36,176 (proposed June 25, 2014), *available at* http://www.gpo.gov/fdsys/pkg/FR-2014-06-25/pdf/2014-14948.pdf

E. CURRENT FAA ENFORCEMENTS

There have been a few enforcement cases[333] to date but the big one is the Pirker case and this will gives us guidance as to what the FAA thinks.

1. THE PIRKER CASE

A man named Raphael Pirker ("Pirker") was paid to fly his UA, [334] over the University of Virginia's campus to gather aerial photographs and video.[335] Pirker did not have a FAA pilot's certificate and was flying the aircraft from anywhere between 10 feet above the ground to more than 400 feet.[336] The FAA found out about Pirker because he posted the video he shot on YouTube.[337] The FAA claimed that Pirker violated 14 C.F.R. § 91.13 for flying his UA in a "careless or reckless

---

[333] The FAA has sent out many cease and desist orders to individuals operating commercially and conversely individuals have sent letters to the FAA challenging their jurisdiction and authority.

[334] A Ritewing Zephyr weighing around 5 pounds.

[335] Order of Assessment, ¶¶ 1, 6, *Administrator v. Pirker*, No. CP-217, (NTSB filed June 27, 2013) [hereinafter "FAA Order of Assessment"], http://www.wired.com/images_blogs/threatlevel/2014/10/Complaint.pdf

[336] *Id.* at ¶¶ 3, 8.

[337] Gary Mortimer, *Stunt Sheep Don't try this at home: Trappys $10k fine UVA video*, YOUTUBE (Oct. 15, 2013), http://www.youtube.com/watch?v=OZnJeuAja-4

96

manner so as to endanger the life or property of another."[338] For this "reckless" behavior, the FAA was fining Pirker $10,000.

What is interesting to note is that the FAA put in the Order Of Assessment that Pirker was an non-certificated pilot, [339] he was being paid,[340] and that he "failed to take precautions to prevent collision hazards with other aircraft that may have been flying within the vicinity of your aircraft." [341]

The FAA has not made it clear as to why Mr. Pirker's commercial activities play any bearing in the case since he is being prosecuted for a violation of 91.13. The FAA's 2007 Policy expressly forbids commercial UAS activity but the FAA only mentions the commercial activity and does not try to seek enforcement for violating the 2007 Policy's ban on commercial activity.

At one point, Pirker flew *above* 400 feet, in navigable airspace, and this was considered to be acting recklessly by the FAA even though he had a spotter and had live-streaming video from the

---

[338] 14 C.F.R. § 91.13(a).
[339] FAA Order of Assessment, *supra* note 335, at ¶ 3.
[340] FAA Order of Assessment, *supra* note 335, at ¶ 6.
[341] FAA Order of Assessment, *supra* note 335, at ¶ 10.

airplane. The argument that should have been made by the FAA was that the streaming video and the spotter were inadequate to fulfilling regulation § 91.113, "see and avoid" other aircraft. Why was Pirker being charged with a violation of being reckless but not the seeing and avoiding regulation? Was it reckless to use spotters and streaming video?

Furthermore, the FAA did not answer what is this "thing" that Pirker flew? Yes, it is an aircraft but is it a model aircraft? Congress exempted model aircraft from future regulations [342] but Pirker's aircraft could not be classified as a model, as per FAA policy, because Pirker was not acting recreationally. If the aircraft is not a model aircraft, what is it? If it is classified an aircraft, then why did the FAA not *also* seek enforcement against Pirker for failing to register[343] his aircraft or for flying an aircraft in an un-airworthy [344] condition

---

[342] FMRA, *infra* note 233, § 336(b) ("Nothing in this section shall be construed to limit the authority of the Administrator to pursue enforcement action against persons operating model aircraft who endanger the safety of the national airspace system.").

[343] *See* 49 U.S.C. § 44101(a) ("[A] person may operate an aircraft only when the aircraft is registered[.]"); *see also* 14 C.F.R. § 47.1("This part prescribes the requirements for registering aircraft under 49 U.S.C. 44101[.]").

[344] *See* 14 C.F.R. § 91.7(a) ("No person may operate a civil aircraft unless it is in an airworthy condition.").

according to the regulations? The reckless charge seems like picking the low hanging fruit while ignoring the more important questions.

2. THE NTSB RULING ON THE PIRKER CASE

These issues of what Pirker flew and the status of the 2007 policy that bans commercial activity and more were *initially* answered when the NTSB administrative law judge published his decision which stated that (1) Pirker flew a model aircraft and was subject only to *voluntary* compliance with AC 91-57, (2) the term "aircraft" 14 C.F.R. § 1.1 or 49 U.S.C. § 40102(a)(6) is not applicable to model aircraft because the FAA has always excluded model aircraft from the definition of "aircraft," (3) the 2005 policy statement and 2008 policy statement were only for internal use in the FAA and did not provide any authority over model aircraft,[345] (4) the 2007 policy statement is either non-binding or it is a failed attempt at creating a rule under 5 U.S.C. § 553, (5) and that there was no enforceable FAA rule or FAR

---

[345] The NTSB order incorrectly cited a case in footnote 14. It should have read "*Syncor Int'l.. Corp. v. Shalala*, 127 F.3d 90, 94 (D.C. Cir. 1997)." The confusion was created because the name Shalala was in the case name for both cases. *Syncor International Corporation. v. Shalala* was the correct case name while *Professionals & Patients for Customized Care v. Shalala* was the case cited. *See infra* note 346, at 5 n14.

regulation that applied to model aircraft or classified model aircraft as UA.[346]

3. THE PROCEDURAL HISTORY OF THE ENFORCEMENT

Pirker was not a certificated pilot so the FAA started seeking to assess a civil penalty against him for $10,000 for acting as a pilot[347] by sending Pirker a notice of Assessment.[348] The attorney for Pirker appealed the enforcement to an administrative law judge ("ALJ") in the National Transportation Safety Board ("NTSB").[349] The attorney for Pirker filed a Motion to Dismiss.[350] The attorney for the FAA filed a response.[351] The attorney for Pirker filed a reply in further support of the Motion to Dismiss[352] and the attorney for the FAA filed a response

---

[346] See Decisional Order, 7-8, *Administrator v. Pirker*, No. CP-217, (NTSB filed June 27, 2013) [hereinafter "NTSB Judgment"], http://www.kramerlevin.com/files/upload/PirkerDecision.pdf

[347] See 49 U.S.C. § 46301(d)(2); *see also* 14 C.F.R. § 13.18(a).

[348] See *id.* at § 13.18(d).

[349] FAA Order of Assessment, *supra* note 328; 49 C.F.R. § 821.2 (It must be noted that the FAA originally filed pursuant § 821.54-57 but later responded to Pirker's Motion to Dismiss under § 821.17.)

[350] Respondent's Motion to Dismiss, *Administrator v. Pirker*, No. CP-217, (NTSB filed June 27, 2013) [hereinafter "Pirker's Motion to Dismiss"], http://www.kramerlevin.com/files/upload/FAA-v-Pirker.pdf; 49 U.S.C. § 821.17(a).

[351] Administrator's Response to Respondent's Motion to Dismiss, *Administrator v. Pirker*, No. CP-217, (NTSB filed June 27, 2013) [hereinafter FAA's Response], http://www.suasnews.com/wp-content/uploads/2013/11/FAA_Response.pdf

[352] Respondent's Reply Memorandum of Law in Further Support of His Motion to Dismiss, *Administrator v. Pirker*, No. CP-217, (NTSB filed June 27, 2013)

to the reply.[353] The NTSB judge gave an initial determination.[354] The day after the NTSB decision, the FAA gave notice that it planned to file an appeal of the decision[355] to the full NTSB board. The FAA's filing of an appeal stayed the lower NTSB judge's initial determination.[356] The FAA filed an appellate brief, [357]Pirker replied,[358] and the Full NTSB Board overruled the lower judge and remanded the case back down to the lower judge.[359]

Since the full NTSB issued its decision on November 17, 2014, either party may appeal to the Federal Circuit Court of Appeals in the District of Columbia.[360] After the DC Appeals Court rules, either party

---

[hereinafter "Pirker's Response to FAA's Response"], http://www.kramerlevin.com/files/upload/PirkerReply.pdf

[353] Administrator's Response to Respondent's Reply in Further Support of His Motion to Dismiss, *Administrator v. Pirker*, No. CP-217, (NTSB filed June 27, 2013) [hereinafter "FAA's Final Response to Pirker's Response"], http://www.suasnews.com/wp-content/uploads/2013/12/FAAFinalReply.pdf

[354] Decisional Order, *supra* note 346;

[355] *See* Press Release, FAA, (March 7, 2014), http://www.faa.gov/news/press_releases/news_story.cfm?newsId=15894&cid=TW209

[356] *See* 49 C.F.R § 821.43.

[357] Administrator's Appeal Brief, *Huerta v. Pirker*, No. CP-217, (NTSB Apr. 14, 2014), *available at* https://app.ntsb.gov/legal/pirker/Administrator'sAppealBrief.pdf

[358] Respondent's Reply Brief, *Huerta v. Pirker*, No. CP-217, (NTSB May 12, 2014), *available at* https://app.ntsb.gov/legal/pirker/Respondent'sReplyBrief.pdf

[359] *See Huerta v. Pirker*, No. CP-217, (NTSB Nov.18, 2014), *available at* https://app.ntsb.gov/legal/pirker/5730.pdf

[360] *See* 49 U.S.C. § 1153(b)-(c).

can appeal to the United States Supreme Court by way of a writ of certiorari.[361]

4. THE ISSUE NOT ANSWERED BY JUDGE GERAGHTY

One of the important questions in this case was not answered; why does the FAA have jurisdiction over this small UA *below* navigable airspace to protect people on the ground when that is not found anywhere in any statutes or regulations? In the FAA's Response to Pirker's Motion to Dismiss, the FAA said, "[t]he FAA unquestionably has authority to regulate aircraft in U.S. airspace" [362] because "§ 40103(b)(1) states that "[t]he Administrator of the Federal Aviation Administration shall develop plans and policy for the use of the navigable airspace *and assign by regulation or order the use of the airspace necessary to ensure the safety of aircraft and the efficient use of airspace.*" [363] Congress set the FAA's jurisdiction to navigable airspace. The FAA defined navigable airspace.

Furthermore, the FAA's Response to Pirker's Motion to Dismiss said, "the legislative history of the Federal Aviation Act of 1958

---

[361] *See* 49 U.S.C. § 1153(b)(5), *see also id.* § 46110(e).
[362] FAA's Response, *supra* note 351, at 2.
[363] *Id.* at 5.

demonstrates, Congress proposed to 'give the Administrator authority to regulate the use of *all airspace* over the United States by both civil and military aircraft. . . .'"[364] The FAA's Response is incorrect. The court in *United States v. Christensen* was referring to the context of events which led to the Federal Aviation Act which was:

> [A] series of 'fatal air crashes between civil and military aircraft operating under separate flight rules . . . . Thus, . . . [the Act's] principal purpose is to create and enforce one unified system of flight rules . . . . [T]he House bill proposed to 'give the Administrator authority to regulate the use of both civil and military aircraft, and to establish and operate a unified system of air-traffic.[365]

The Federal Aviation Act was "to make all aircraft subject to the air traffic rules . . . ."[366] Context tells us that the "all airspace" is referring to the airspace where military and civil aircraft would interact, not all airspace everywhere. Congress could have said "all airspace" so as to include airspace below navigable airspace but instead said "navigable airspace" when it defined the FAA's jurisdiction. A good phrase to remember when looking at the word "all" in context is: all does not

---

[364] FAA's Response, *supra* note 351, at 5 (quoting *United States v. Christenson*, 419 F.2d 1401, 1404 (9th Cir. 1969)).
[365] *United States v. Christensen*, 419 F.2d 1401, 1404 (9th Cir. 1969).
[366] *Id.* at 1404.

mean *all*, all the time. Furthermore, the FMRA said "national airspace" as opposed to "navigable airspace." Did that matter?

Moreover, the FAA gave one last justification for its jurisdiction below navigable airspace by saying that the FAA can create regulations for the flight of aircraft for "navigating, protecting, and identifying aircraft" and "protecting individuals on the ground,"[367] along with citing a case that said, "persons on the ground[.]"[368] The FAA could have bolstered that argument, but did not, by saying that navigable airspace has out of necessity descended all the way to the ground because technology has rapidly changed to allow small UA to now operate close to the ground and in between buildings before regulations have been properly created. The FAA could have listed the many things that are below navigable airspace that are regulated such as those things listed earlier in this book.

Finally, by appealing the initial decision, the FAA potentially risked the full NTSB board ruling on the navigable airspace issue. The full NTSB board has the ability to change the initial ruling and issue

---

[367] 49 U.S.C. § 40103(b)(2).
[368] *City of Burbank v. Lockheed Air Terminal Inc.*, 411 U.S. 624, 638-39 (1973).

104

an order of its own.[369] The FAA could have made the decision to not appeal the case which would have made the case only binding upon the FAA and Pirker in this particular case but not on future FAA enforcements.[370]

5. THE FULL NTSB BOARD MAKES A RULING

On November 17th, 2014, the full NTSB board held that the drone that Pirker did fly was an "airplane."[371] The Board applied the "rules of construction to interpret [the] statutes and regulations. If the language of a provision is clear and unambiguous on its face, the language controls; if the language is ambiguous, [the Board] interpret[s] the provision in reference to, among other factors, the context in which it appears."[372] The Board stated:

> The definitions are clear on their face[373] . . . . [and they] do not exclude even a 'model aircraft' from the meaning of 'aircraft.' Furthermore, the definitions draw no distinction between whether a device is manned or unmanned. An aircraft is 'any' 'device' that is 'used for flight.' We acknowledge the

---

[369] *See* 49 C.F.R. § 821.49.
[370] *See* 49 C.F.R. § 821.43.
[371] *See Huerta v. Pirker*, CP-217, page 5 of pdf (NTSB filed Nov. 18, 2014) [hereinafter "NTSB Board Decision"], http://www.ntsb.gov/legal/alj/OnODocuments/Aviation/5730.pdf
[372] *Id.* at 4 (footnotes omitted).
[373] *Id.* at 5.

definitions are as broad as they are clear, but they are clear nonetheless.[374]

Thus, "the law judge erred in presuming the regulations categorically do not apply to model aircraft." [375] The Board concluded that the regulation which prohibits careless and reckless operation, Section 91.13(a), "applies with respect to the operation of any 'aircraft' other than those subject to parts 101 and 103" and the case should be remanded "to the law judge for a full factual hearing to determine whether [Pirker] operated the aircraft 'in a careless or reckless manner[.]'"[376]

6. THE PIRKER CASE SETTLES

On January 22, 2015, the Pirker case came to an end by the FAA agreeing to drop the case in exchange for Pirker paying a $1,100 fine which "does not constitute an admission of any allegations in this case or an admission of any regulatory violation."[377]

The decision to settle the case was not an easy one, but the length of time that would be needed to pursue further

---

[374] *Id.* at 5-6 (footnotes omitted).
[375] *Id.* at 7.
[376] *Id.* at 12.
[377] Team BlackSheep Drone Pilot Raphael Pirker Settles FAA Case, 1, http://www.scribd.com/doc/253446698/Pirker-Faa-Settlement

proceedings and appeals, and the FAA's new reliance on a statute that post-dates Raphael's flight, have diminished the utility of the case to assist the commercial drone industry in its regulatory struggle.[378]

The drone industry has felt the effects of the case. For one, "It not only prompted a vigorous international public discussion about the existing framework, but also has encouraged regulators to open new paths forward."

There was still a big question left unanswered. Were Pirker's actions reckless? Brendan Schulman, the attorney for Pirker, thinks he knows the answer to the question, "The regulation requires endangerment of life or the property of another. If they found the risk was giving someone a scratch, there's certainly the possibility it would have established that flying a styrofoam model in and of itself doesn't pose the kind of danger to people necessary to meet the regulatory standard."[379]

---

[378] *Id.* at 1.

[379] Jason Koebler, *The Commercial Drone Pilot Who Ruined the FAA's 2014 Has Settled His Case*, MOTHERBOARD (Jan. 22, 2015), http://motherboard.vice.com/read/the-commercial-drone-pilot-who-ruined-the-faas-2014-has-settled-his-case

F. NON-FAA ENFORCEMENT PROBLEMS

The National Park Service ("NPS") has started cracking down on unmanned aircraft operators. The NPS issued a press release that the director of NPS "signed a policy memorandum that directs superintendents nationwide to prohibit launching, landing, or operating unmanned aircraft on lands and waters administered by the National Park Service."[380] "The policy memorandum directs park superintendents to take a number of steps to exclude unmanned aircraft from national parks. The steps include drafting a written justification for the action, ensuring compliance with applicable laws, and providing public notice of the action."[381] "The policy memo directs superintendents to use their existing authority within the Code of Federal Regulations to prohibit the use of unmanned aircraft, and to include that prohibition in the park's compendium, a set of park-specific regulations."[382] This press release seems to be in response to the confusion caused by multiple parks issuing different statements

---

[380] Press Release, Nat'l Park Serv., Unmanned Aircraft to be Prohibited in America's National Parks (June 20, 2014), *available at* http://home.nps.gov/news/release.htm?id=1601

[381] *Id.*

[382] *Id.*

about drone use[383] and Professor Greg McNeal pointing out the absurd legal arguments of Yosemite National Park using current NPS regulations to prohibit unmanned aircraft. [384] The NPS policy memorandum calls for closure of NPS lands and waters under 36 C.F.R. § 1.5 while admitting Professor McNeal was right, though not directly, by saying:

> [The] reason for the required closures is that current NPS regulations do not specifically address launching, landing, or operating unmanned aircraft. The prohibition on operating or using an aircraft in 36 CFR 2.17(a)(1) does not apply to unmanned aircraft because the definition of "aircraft" in 36 CFR 1.4 is limited to devices used or intended to be used for human flight. Further, section 2.17(a)(3) could be construed to apply only to unmanned aircraft when used to deliver or retrieve an object from NPS-administered lands. . . . Because the existing NPS regulations can only be used to address unmanned aircraft in certain circumstances, the best way at this time for superintendents to address the use of unmanned aircraft is to exercise their authority pursuant to 36 CFR 1.5.[385]

---

[383] See Greg S. McNeal, *Six Months In Jail For Drones In Parks, According To What Law?*, FORBES (May 5, 2014) http://www.forbes.com/sites/gregorymcneal/2014/05/05/park-service-ignores-law-says-flying-a-drone-may-mean-six-months-in-jail-5000-fine/

[384] See Greg S. McNeal, *Yosemite Looks To Ban Drones By Relying On An Absurd Legal Argument*, FORBES (May 3, 2014), http://www.forbes.com/sites/gregorymcneal/2014/05/03/yosemite-looks-to-ban-drones-but-the-law-is-not-on-their-side/

[385] NAT'L PARK SERV., Policy Memorandum 14-05, Unmanned Aircraft – Interim Policy (2014), *available at* http://www.nps.gov/policy/PolMemos/PM_14-05.htm

However, this is not a complete ban because some limited flying is allowed under strict conditions as set forth in the "Conditions and Exceptions" section of the memorandum. Also, in the frequently asked questions portion, it says:

Does it matter where an unmanned aircraft is used for the required closures to apply?

Yes. The NPS has the authority to regulate or prohibit the use of unmanned aircraft from or on lands and waters administered by the NPS. As a result, the compendium closures required by the Policy Memorandum only apply to launching, landing, or operating unmanned aircraft from or on lands and waters administered by the NPS within the boundaries of the park. The closures do not apply to launching, landing, or operating unmanned aircraft from or on non-federally (e.g., private or state) owned lands located within the exterior boundaries of the park. The closures do not apply to the flight of unmanned aircraft in the airspace above a park if the device is launched, landed, and operated from or on lands and waters that are not administered by the NPS.[386]

The memorandum goes on to provide: (1) some examples of NPS regulations that unmanned aircraft could violate in exhibit A, (2) guidelines on allowing unmanned aircraft operation in exhibit B, and (3) a frequently asked questions section in exhibit C.[387]

---

[386] *See id.* at Frequently Asked Question 9 in Exhibit C.
[387] *See id.*

So why in the world did I include this chapter right after the Pirker case? It is because Pirker was flying his unmanned aircraft at Grand Canyon National Park back in December of 2011 (about two months after the University of Virginia incident) and "Park rangers approached him, demanded he ground the drone and that he delete any footage he took. Pirker turned over his drone's memory card, but only after rangers threatened to obtain a search warrant to seize it, according to a citation report."[388] Pirker was fined $325 based upon violating 36 C.F.R. § 2.17, the same section later viewed to not be applicable to unmanned aircraft according to NPS memorandum.[389] The Assistant United States Attorney for the citation, in an email, told Pirker:

> [S]hould you desire to contest this citation, we can set the matter for trial, and you can return to the Grand Canyon . . . . [Y]ou have the option of paying by mail the collateral forfeiture amount ($325) indicated on the face of the ticket. If you choose this option, the matter is treated as a civil matter and does not result in any criminal conviction. If however you proceed to trial and are convicted, the resulting conviction

---

[388] Jason Koebler, *Feds Confiscated a Hobbyist's Drone Footage to Keep It Off the Internet*, MOTHERBOARD (May 6, 2014), http://motherboard.vice.com/en_uk/read/feds-confiscated-a-hobbyists-drone-footage-to-keep-it-off-the-internet

[389] *See id.*

would be considered a Class B misdemeanor, punishable by up to six months jail and/or a $5,000 fine.[390]

So here is the conclusion to the section, whether the FAA or NPS is wrong or right, there is a personal cost to all of this by "taking a ride through the system." There is what the law IS, and there is what the FAA thinks the law is – the second one is what matters.

---

[390] *See id.*

112

CHAPTER EIGHT: HOW TO LEGALLY OPERATE YOUR MODEL AIRCRAFT

This section covers the guidance material from the FAA and also the regulations that the FAA believes apply to model aircraft.

A. MODEL AIRCRAFT GUIDANCE MATERIAL

So how does one fly their model aircraft without getting into trouble? The FAA has some guidance on this topic. The FAA issued their (1) Interpretation of the Special Rule for Model Aircraft,[391] (2) Law Enforcement Guidance for Suspected Unauthorized UAS Operations,[392] (3) the Know Before You Fly campaign,[393] (4) "What Can I Do With My Model Aircraft?" webpage on the FAA's

---

[391] *See* 2014 Model Aircraft Policy Statement, *supra* note 220.
[392] *See* LEA Guidance, *supra* note 313.
[393] *Recreational Users*, http://knowbeforeyoufly.org/for-recreational-users/ (It was "founded by the Association for Unmanned Vehicle Systems International (AUVSI), the Academy of Model Aeronautics (AMA), and the Small UAV Coalition in partnership with the Federal Aviation Administration (FAA)").

website,[394] and (5) Advisory Circular 91-57.[395] The following list is synthesized from all the material and will have a number assigned to it to indicate where it came from because some of the guidance is not consistent throughout all of the material. This list covers **ONLY** the FAA and **does not cover state, city, or town laws** which could prohibit flying. Please keep in mind that this list might become outdated and you should check with your local AMA field and/or an aviation attorney prior to any flight.

Compilation of Model Aircraft Guidelines

The aircraft is flown strictly for **hobby or recreational** use. You can't make money off the flying incidentally. Sources: (1),(2),(4).
The aircraft is operated in accordance with a **community-based set of safety guidelines** and within the programming of a nationwide community-based organization. Sources: (1),(2),(3).
The aircraft is limited to not more than **55 pounds [Take Off Weight]** unless otherwise certified through a design, construction, inspection, flight test, and operational safety program administered by a community-based organization. Sources: (1),(2),(4).
The aircraft is operated in a manner that **does not interfere** with and gives way to any **manned aircraft**. See also § 91.113. Sources: (1),(2),(3),(4),(5).
When flown within **5 miles** of an airport, the operator of the

---

[394] *What Can I Do With My Model Aircraft? Hobby/Recreational Flying*, FED. AVIATION ADMIN. [hereinafter "Model Webpage"], http://www.faa.gov/uas/publications/model_aircraft_operators/
[395] *See supra* note 126.

aircraft provides the **airport operator and the airport air traffic control tower** (when an air traffic facility is located at the airport) with **prior notice** of the operation (model aircraft operators flying from a permanent location within 5 miles of an airport should establish a mutually-agreed upon operating procedure with the airport operator and the airport air traffic control tower (when an air traffic facility is located at the airport)). AC 91-57 said 3 miles. Sources: (1),(2),(3),(4).

Do not fly your model in a "**careless or reckless manner** so as to endanger the life or property of another." Sources: (2); Section 336(c) of the FMRA; 14 C.F.R. § 91.13.

Do not fly the aircraft beyond **visual line-of-sight**. Sources: (1),(3),(4), FRMA § 336(c)(2).

"The aircraft must be **visible at all times** to the operator[.]"Source: (1).

"[T]he operator must use his or her own **natural vision** (which includes vision corrected by standard eyeglasses or contact lenses) to observe the aircraft." You cannot use "vision-enhancing devices, such as binoculars, night vision goggles, powered vision magnifying devices, and goggles designed to provide a 'first-person view' from the model." Source: (1).

"[P]eople other than the operator may not be used in lieu of the operator for maintaining visual line of sight." **No daisy chain**. Source: (1).

The FAA mentioned in their Model Rule Interpretation § 91.119(c) which says do not operate the aircraft in a non-congested area "closer than **500 feet** to any person, vessel, vehicle, or structure." Model aircraft "may still pose a risk to persons and property on the ground warranting enforcement action when **conducted unsafely**." However, in the Know Before You Fly campaign which the FAA partnered with, it says, "Do not intentionally fly over unprotected persons or moving vehicles, and remain at least **25 feet** away from individuals and vulnerable property." **This distance requirement is unclear.** Sources: (1) and/or? (3).

Fly no higher than **400 feet** above ground level and remain below

any surrounding obstacles when possible. Sources: (3),(5).
The "operating site that is of **sufficient distance from populated areas.** The selected site should be away from noise sensitive areas such as parks, schools, hospitals, churches, etc." Source: (5).
"Do not operate model aircraft in the presence of spectators until the aircraft is **successfully flight tested and proven airworthy**." Source: (5).
"Do not fly in **adverse weather** conditions such as in high winds or reduced visibility." Source: (3).
"Do not fly under the influence of **alcohol or drugs**." Source: (3).
"Do not fly **near or over sensitive infrastructure or property** such as power stations, water treatment facilities, correctional facilities, heavily traveled roadways, government facilities, etc." Source: (3).
"Check and follow all **local laws** and ordinances before flying over private property." Source: (3).
"Do not conduct **surveillance or photograph** persons in areas where there is an **expectation of privacy** without the individual's permission." Source: (3).
Note: Keep in the **National Park Service** restrictions!

B. FEDERAL AVIATION REGULATIONS THAT THE FAA BELIEVES APPLY TO MODEL AIRCRAFT

While the FAA has provided guidance specifically to model aircraft, the FAA has incorporated by reference sections of the Federal Aviation Regulations that they believe apply to model aircraft. The FAA breaks the regulations down "into three categories: (1) how the aircraft is operated; (2) operating rules for designated airspace; and, (3) special restrictions such as temporary flight restrictions (TFRs) and notices to airmen (NOTAMs)."[396] "These rules are the baseline rules that apply to all aircraft operated in the United States with limited exceptions[397] and are the appropriate rules to apply when evaluating model aircraft operations."[398]

> Other rules in part 91, or other parts of the regulations, may apply to model aircraft operations, depending on the particular circumstances of the operation. The regulations cited [below] are not intended to be an exhaustive list of rules that could apply to model aircraft operations. The FAA anticipates that the cited regulations are the ones that would most commonly apply to model aircraft operations.[399]

1. MODEL AIRCRAFT OPERATING REGULATIONS.

§ 91.13 Careless or reckless operation.

> (a) Aircraft operations for the purpose of air navigation. No person may operate an aircraft in a careless or reckless manner so as to endanger the life or property of another.
>
> (b) Aircraft operations other than for the purpose of air navigation. No person may operate an aircraft, other than for the purpose of air navigation, on any part of the surface of an airport used by aircraft for air commerce (including

---

[396] 2014 Model Aircraft Policy Statement, *supra* note 220, at 36,175.
[397] "Part 91 does not apply to moored balloons, kites, unmanned rockets, and unmanned free balloons, and ultralights vehicles operated under 14 CFR parts 101 and 103." *Id.*
[398] *Id.*
[399] *Id.* at 36,176.

areas used by those aircraft for receiving or discharging persons or cargo), in a careless or reckless manner so as to endanger the life or property of another.

§ 91.15 Dropping objects.

No pilot in command of a civil aircraft may allow any object to be dropped from that aircraft in flight that creates a hazard to persons or property. However, this section does not prohibit the dropping of any object if reasonable precautions are taken to avoid injury or damage to persons or property.

§ 91.113 Right-of-way rules: Except water operations.

(a) *Inapplicability.* This section does not apply to the operation of an aircraft on water.

(b) *General.* When weather conditions permit, regardless of whether an operation is conducted under instrument flight rules or visual flight rules, vigilance shall be maintained by each person operating an aircraft so as to see and avoid other aircraft. When a rule of this section gives another aircraft the right-of-way, the pilot shall give way to that aircraft and may not pass over, under, or ahead of it unless well clear.

(c) *In distress.* An aircraft in distress has the right-of-way over all other air traffic.

(d) *Converging.* When aircraft of the same category are converging at approximately the same altitude (except head-on, or nearly so), the aircraft to the other's right has the right-of-way. If the aircraft are of different categories—

(1) A balloon has the right-of-way over any other category of aircraft;

(2) A glider has the right-of-way over an airship, powered parachute, weight-shift-control aircraft, airplane, or rotorcraft.

(3) An airship has the right-of-way over a powered parachute, weight-shift-control aircraft, airplane, or rotorcraft.

However, an aircraft towing or refueling other aircraft has the right-of-way over all other engine-driven aircraft.

(e) *Approaching head-on.* When aircraft are approaching each other head-on, or nearly so, each pilot of each aircraft shall alter course to the right.

(f) *Overtaking.* Each aircraft that is being overtaken has the right-of-way and each pilot of an overtaking aircraft shall alter course to the right to pass well clear.

(g) *Landing.* Aircraft, while on final approach to land or while landing, have the right-of-way over other aircraft in flight or operating on the surface, except that they shall not take advantage of this rule to force an aircraft off the runway surface which has already landed and is attempting to make way for an aircraft on final approach. When two or more aircraft are approaching an airport for the purpose of landing, the aircraft at the lower altitude has the right-of-way, but it shall not take advantage of this rule to cut in front of another which is on final approach to land or to overtake that aircraft.

"Model aircraft that do not comply with [these] rules could be subject to [an] FAA enforcement action."[400]

2. OPERATING RULES FOR DESIGNATED AIRSPACE.

This section will not be quoting the regulations but only the titles.

Please check over these regulations before you operate. The FAA explained in the 2014 Model Rule Interpretation that the operating rules for designated airspace:

---

[400] *Id.*

[A]re found in §§ 91.126 through 91.135. In general, those rules establish requirements for operating in the various classes of airspace, and near airports in nondesignated airspace to minimize risk of collision in higher traffic airspace. Generally, if an operator is unable to comply with the regulatory requirements for operating in a particular class of airspace, the operator would need authorization from air traffic control to operate in that area. See, e.g., 14 CFR 91.127(a), 91.129(a). [401]

Designated Airspace Regulations

91.126	Operating on or in the vicinity of an airport in Class G airspace.
91.127	Operating on or in the vicinity of an airport in Class E airspace.
91.129	Operations in Class D airspace.
91.130	Operations in Class C airspace.
91.131	Operations in Class B airspace.
91.133	Restricted and prohibited areas.
91.135	Operations in Class A airspace.

In addition to these airspace regulations, the FAA also addressed special use airspace (restricted and prohibited areas) by saying:

Operations within restricted areas designated in part 73 would be prohibited without permission from the using or controlling agency. Accordingly, as part of the requirements for model aircraft operations within miles of an airport set forth in section 336(a)(4) of [the FMRA], the FAA would expect modelers operating model aircraft in airspace covered by §§ 91.126 through 91.135 and part 73 to obtain authorization from air traffic control prior to operating. [402]

---

[401] *Id.*
[402] *Id.*

3. SPECIAL RESTRICTIONS SUCH AS TEMPORARY FLIGHT RESTRICTIONS AND NOTICES TO AIRMEN.

This section will not be quoting the regulations but only the titles. **Please check over these regulations before you operate.** You can find out of there is a TFR by going to http://tfr.faa.gov/tfr2/list.html or calling 1-800-WX-BRIEF (992-7433) and asking if there are any TFR's currently active or will become active TFR's at your location.

91.137	Temporary flight restrictions in the vicinity of disaster/hazard areas.
91.138	Temporary flight restrictions in national disaster areas in the State of Hawaii.
91.139	Emergency air traffic rules.
91.141	Flight restrictions in the proximity of the Presidential and other parties.
91.143	Flight limitation in the proximity of space flight operations.
91.144	Temporary restriction on flight operations during abnormally high barometric pressure conditions.
91.145	Management of aircraft operations in the vicinity of aerial demonstrations and major sporting events.

CHAPTER NINE: THE FUTURE OF UNMANNED AIRCRAFT

There will definitely be a future, but the question is how regulated will it be? Judging from the 2013 Roadmap, unmanned pilots will be required to have some type of pilot's certificate and medical certificate. There will be provisions in place for "quickly" obtaining a SAC-EC, SAC-RC, 333's, or COA's. At some point, regulations for sUAS operations will be created. Those regulations still have to be published in the Federal Register and commented on before the FAA can publish the final rule. Finally, privacy issues are going to cause many roadblocks going forward.

DISCUSSION QUESTIONS

I. What are some of your concerns about UA?

II.

  A.

    1. What do you think we should call these aircraft and why?

    2. Is there a difference between an unmanned aircraft and a remotely piloted aircraft?

  B.

    1. How many ways do you think UA can save lives?

    2. UA might cause deaths, but do you think more lives will be saved than lost?

    3. Can you think of an example of how a UA could have saved someone's life if it had been used?

    4. Of the civilian uses listed, which do you feel is the most Important? Which is the easiest to implement? Which is the safest?

    5. Of the government uses, which do you feel is the most important?

6. Does it bother you to know that police have the ability to watch you with a drone? Do you think they should be required to have search warrants?

7. Does it seem inconsistent when individuals say that it is permissible for police to have helicopters but not drones? Why?

C.

1. How will drones have an economic impact?

2. Have drones had an economic impact even though they are being hindered by regulations?

3. How will drones create jobs?

4. Which is larger, the amount of money saved by drones or the amount of money created by drone based jobs? Which is more important?

5. Which sector will stand to save the most money using drones?

6. Which sector will make the most money using drones?

7. Give me an example of a job that was created by drone technology that would not have been there before with manned aircraft.

8. Let's say that drones never save lives directly, do you think that the amount of lives saved by increasing crop yields will be more than the lives lost due to drone crashes?

9. Why are drones better for crop monitoring than planes and satellites?

10. How much damage is done to the environment by prophylactically spraying everything everywhere with herbicides, pesticides, and fungicides than by allowing drones to do precision spraying? Don't you think the Environmental Protection Agency and other environmental groups should be making a large push for the integration of this technology? Why do you think they have not been?

11. Police helicopters cost money to fly and maintain. Do you think there is a good argument for the immediate implementation of drones in the police force to lower the operating budget of the police?

12. How likely do you think it is for a jet liner to crash because of a drone? Why?

13. If most commercial aircraft have two or more engines and two pilots, how would one drone cause the commercial aircraft to crash?

14. Can you think of a scenario?

15. How likely is that scenario to happen as opposed to bird strikes?

16. Don't you think we should focus more on preventing bird strikes especially when a flock of birds took out both engines on the U.S. Airways jet that crashed into the Hudson River?

III.

B.

1. Discuss the term "Navigable Airspace."

2. Is the airspace between buildings in New York City navigable airspace?

3. Based upon the *Causby* case, make an argument where terrestrial property rights end.

4. How far does the FAA's authority extend down to? Why is it a good idea to have the FAA control airspace all the way down to the ground? Why is it a bad idea?

5. How many types of airspace are there? Why do you think there are so many? Why does the Class B airport look like an upside down wedding cake?

C.

1. What does the FAA regulate?

2. What is the FAA's definition of an aircraft? Could a baseball, Frisbee, golf ball, or paper airplane be an "aircraft?"

3. In your opinion, is a UA really an aircraft according to the FARs?

4. How does the FAA create a regulation?

5. What is a grant of exemption?

6. Explain a Section 333 exemption.

7. What are the main types of documents the FAA publishes in addition to the FARs?

8. Does a policy statement carry the same regulatory authority as the FAR's?

9. What is the procedure for obtaining a SAC-EC?

10. Why was the 2007 Policy Statement created?

11. Are business purposes and commercial operations the same?

12. In the 2008 Policy Statement, do you think it is fair for the FAA to require a second class medical certificate?

13. List the prohibited uses of model aircraft in the 2014 "Interpretive Rule." Do you agree with them?

IV.

1. What is the purpose of the FMRA?

2. What is Section 333 of the FMRA and why is it important?

3. What happens if the FAA misses deadlines?

V.

1. Do you think the FAA Roadmap is subject to change?

VI.

1. What are the six ways a UA may be operated in the NAS?

A.

1. What is a COA and does it only apply to public aircraft?

2. What is a public aircraft? What is a civil aircraft?

3. Explain the two types of COA's for public aircraft.

B.

1. What are the differences between a SAC-EC and a SAC-RC?

128

2. Where is the line between commercial civil aircraft and model aircraft? Is there a third category of non-commercial and non-model aircraft? What would that be?

C.

1. Explain how the FAA judges a 333 petition. What does a petitioner have to answer?

VII.

B.

1. What is one reason why certificated pilots are hesitant to fly unmanned aircraft commercially?

C.

1. Would you risk a $10,000 fine to make some money?

D.

1. What do you see as reckless flying by an unmanned aircraft? Give some examples.

E.

1. How does the FAA encourage compliance with the regulations?
2. How does the FAA use local law enforcement to enforce prohibited UA operations?
3. Discuss the outcome of the Pirker case on the future likelihood of prohibited commercial UA operations.
4. Was Pirker's actions reckless? How would you have ruled?

5. Why do you think Judge Geraghty didn't answer the jurisdictional question? Do you agree with the NTSB's ruling on appeal?

6. Do you think the case should have settled?

F.

1. Do you think Pirker should have fought the citation?

2. What do you think of the NPS not allowing drones to be flown in the parks? Could they have done this another way?

VIII.

A.

1. Why is it important to check local laws before flying?

2. Do you think the guidance is confusing? Why?

3. Which of the parts of guidance do you agree with? Which do you not agree with? Why?

4. Do you think FPV could actually enhance safety?

B.

1. Do you find it confusing that model aircraft operators are going to have to read and comply with regulations?

2. Do you think that model aircraft can or cannot easily comply with these regulations?

IX.

1. What do you think will be the most important uses of UA in the future?

2. What are the major hurdles going forward?

ONE LAST THING

Thank you for reading my book! If this book was helpful to you, I would appreciate it if you post a short review on Amazon. I read your reviews so I can get your feedback to make the book even better for future readers. If you have ideas for a future book, let me know by emailing me at jon@jrupprechtlaw.com

Thanks!